JAMES G. BENNETT has been a mental health counselor in private practice since 1952 and has worked with amateur athletes, coaches, World Class, Olympic, and professional athletes. The founder and president of Human Factors Seminars, Inc., he developed Mental Dynamics for Athletes, a complete course in sports psychology.

JAMES E. PRAVITZ is an analytical account manager for the Boeing Commercial Sales Department. In addition to participating in sports all his life, he is a lay practitioner of sports psychology and has written several articles on the subject of sports.

JAMES G. BENNETT
JAMES E. PRAVITZ

The Miracle of SPORTS Psychology

A SPECTRUM BOOK

PRENTICE-HALL, INC., Englewood Cliffs, N.J. 07632

Library of Congress Cataloging in Publication Data

Bennett, James Gordon.
    The miracle of sports psychology

    Includes index.
    1. Sports—Psychological aspects.   I. Pravitz,
James E.   II. Title.
GV706.4.B46   796'.01   82-5324
ISBN 0-13-585257-9   AACR2
ISBN 0-13-585240-4 (pbk.)

This book is available at a special discount when ordered in large quantities.
Contact Prentice-Hall, Inc., General Publishing Division,
Special Sales, Englewood Cliffs, N. J. 07632.

A SPECTRUM BOOK

10   9   8   7   6   5   4   3   2   1

Printed in the United States of America

Editorial/production supervision: Marlys Lehmann
Manufacturing buyer: Barbara A. Frick
Cover and jacket design: Jeannette Jacobs
Cover illustration: April Blair Stewart

ISBN 0-13-585257-9

ISBN 0-13-585240-4 {PBK.}

Prentice-Hall International, Inc., *London*
Prentice-Hall of Australia Pty. Limited, *Syndey*
Prentice-Hall Canada, Inc., *Toronto*
Prentice-Hall of India Private Limited, *New Delhi*
Prentice-Hall of Japan, Inc., *Tokyo*
Prentice-Hall of Southeast Asia Pte Ltd., *Singapore*
Whitehall Books Limited, *Wellington, New Zealand*
Editora Prentice-Hall do Brasil LTDA., *Rio de Janeiro*

Contents

Acknowledgments

Our thanks to Bill Griffith, Canadian White Water Champion, whose enthusiasm, encouragement, and prompting got this project started.

And thanks to Carolyn Johnson—researcher, typist, and proofreader—who introduced the authors to one another and became a vital part of the writing team for this book.

Preface

The Miracle of Sports Psychology is the end product of an evolutionary process that began thirty years ago. At that time James Bennett started his career
as a counselor, helping people to sort out the myriad problems of life.

In time he found that the desire for personal improvement was universal among his clients, no matter whether they wished to advance on their
jobs, overcome depression, find more satisfaction in marriage, or excel
as an athlete. What's more, it became apparent that certain techniques for
dealing with—and changing—mental attitudes and mental processes formed a
common denominator that allowed people to take control of their lives and
to assume a position of responsibility for their own growth by learning how
to tap into the incredible mental resources within each of us.

In later years Bennett dealt more and more with athletes who wanted
to overcome mental barriers that they felt were keeping them from reaching
their potential. Both amateur and professional athletes sought his help, so he
began to document the procedures he had developed for his athletic clients.

By the mid-seventies he was working with Bill Griffith, Canadian
National White Water Slalom Champion. Griffith became so enthusiastic
about what he learned that he encouraged Bennett to write a book on the
subject. Griffith felt the techniques were unique and far better than anything
else he had seen, including the techniques then in use by Iron Curtain athletes
against whom he had competed.

Near the end of 1976 Bennett had completed work on an audio program consisting of six tapes and supplementary workbooks. The program was
titled *Mental Dynamics for Athletes* and became a popular training aide for
both individuals and institutions.

Subsequently, the authors of *The Miracle of Sports Psychology* were introduced and began preliminary work on this book, using the techniques developed for the audio program.

Shortly thereafter, a videotape program was created by filming a group training session whose students included Zaid Abdul Aziz (formerly Don Smith, NBA center), Linda Fernandez (later to become an ABC Superstars champion), Jim Miller (who later set an APBA powerboat speed record), and several others, from high school athletes to professionals. Twelve sports were represented.

The knowledge gained from all these experiences has been incorporated into *The Miracle of Sports Psychology*, which is designed to bring these valuable self-improvement techniques to a larger population of athletes.

A side benefit is the fact that these same techniques can be used in other areas of life, not just in sports. That idea can be summed up by paraphrasing William Jennings Bryant: "Success in sports and life is not a matter of chance. It is a choice."

Most people sense this truth but are frustrated in their attempts to implement that choice successfully. This book has been written with that in mind, and makes additional tools available so you can implement your choices and discover how much more there is to your personal capacity for success.

The most fundamental tool that we have to achieve our choices is the mind. Though this is obvious, there is still much frustration until you learn how to use your mind. Everyone tells us to "use your head," but who tells us *how*? That's right—no one.

But now you will know how, because *The Miracle of Sports Psychology* will show you the techniques needed to use your brain effectively and intentionally and will enable you to take the chance factor out of sport and life—and make it your choice.

Foreword

"Are you trying to tell me that it's all in my head?"

That incredulous question is one I hear frequently from my patients. "No," I usually reply, "it's not all in your head. But the roots of part of the problem may be there—and a large part of the solution certainly is!"

In fifteen years of practice as a family and sports physician, the incredible importance of interplay between the activity of the mind and the activity of the body has been demonstrated to me repeatedly. Thus, while prescribing medication, therapeutic devices, special diets, and rehabilitative exercise, I am very likely to suggest changes in a patient's mental attitudes, goals, objectives, thinking habits, and emotional adjustments. I do this while trying to get the patient to understand the relationship between these items and the desired therapeutic result, thereby encouraging the development of the power inherent in the patient's mind, which can be used to maximum advantage for improvement or recovery.

Until recently my prescriptions for harnessing mental power were couched in the generalities used by physicians for generations. While not totally ineffective, they were inconsistent in action and unpredictable in outcome. The key to understanding the intuitive concept of mind-body interaction, and being able to use it effectively, was provided to me about five years ago when I first met James Bennett at a sports medicine symposium. He introduced me to an audio tape album titled "Mental Dynamics for Athletes" which was a system for the use of mental conditioning in the search for athletic success. I quickly realized, after hearing the first tape, that this represented a systematic and applicable approach to what I was trying, in a much less effective way, to convey to patients and athletes for whom I was caring.

I have since gotten to know Jim quite well, have studied his program carefully, and have found that it more than justifies the enthusiasm I felt at that first hearing. The principles of Mental Dynamics now color my interactions with my patients, and I believe that the effect has been a very positive one.

While it is gratifying to see a therapeutic benefit when these principles are applied, it is even more thrilling to view the results when an already good athlete, desiring further improvement, follows the Mental Dynamics for Athletes program in its entirety. As a high school team physician, caring for male and female athletes in all interscholastic sports, I have encouraged several to study and apply the program as presented on tape. In those cases where mental conditioning has been added to the physical conditioning already practiced by the athlete, the results have been spectacular, not only in terms of performance, but in attitude, coachability, resistance to injury, speed of healing, interaction with team members, and personal enjoyment of the sport. Additionally, the athletes seem able to generalize the learned principles and techniques used in athletics, and have often applied them to much wider applications such as academic pursuits, interpersonal relationships, career choice and preparation, and similar important affairs of life.

Those of us involved in sports, or in preparation of athletes for superior performance, or in the prevention or rehabilitation of sports injuries are always searching for the nuance that will make the difference. We study biomechanics and kinesiology, devise new weight-lifting equipment and methods to build strength, propose new programs to develop speed and endurance, manipulate diets, vitamins, and drugs to enhance competitive ability, and spend untold amounts of time and money analyzing shoes, helmets, bats, and other pieces of equipment in a continuing effort to boost performance. In this sometimes frantic search, it amazes me that so little attention has been paid to the role of the athlete's mind in his or her total effort and achievement. Certainly, coaches and athletes are not ignorant of the importance of motivation and goal-orientation, and most give at least some thought to these matters in their team or individual preparation. But the mental aspects of athletics has lacked the defined basic science, the documentation of methodology, and the literature which is available in the fields of physical conditioning and skills development, and has therefore lagged behind in application. It is as a significant step in correcting these deficiencies that I welcome the appearance of the book, *The Miracle of Sports Psychology*, in which James Bennett and James Pravitz have further refined and expanded the principles and methods first presented in the Mental Dynamics for Athletes Tape Program.

I know that *The Miracle of Sports Psychology* will rapidly put this effective approach into the hands and minds of athletes, coaches, trainers, team physicians, and educators with a scope that the tape album, despite its great acceptance, could never accomplish. In doing this, I suspect that the authors are opening the door to athletic achievements that are today considered as "impossible" as the sub-four-minute-mile was prior to Roger Bannister. More important, they are assuring that readers who study and practice the methods presented here will be better at what they choose to do, in or out of athletics, than they would be otherwise—and they will enjoy their sports, and themselves, a great deal more.

Warren B. Howe, M.D., F.A.C.S.M.
Oak Harbor, Washington

1 "Ready, Get Set, Go!"

There ain't no man can avoid being born average. But there ain't no man got to be common.

LEROY ROBERT ("Satchel") Paige[1]

A champion white water racer glides smoothly through the gates of the tumbling course. The weather is chilly, the water near freezing. The hands of his competitors grow stiff and inflexible—their performance suffers. But his hands remain warm and supple, with no covering, and he sweeps on to victory.

How does Canadian Champion Bill Griffith accomplish this? Simply by programming his subconscious mind, a technique he learned from Mental Dynamics principles taught in this book.

Beyond that specific application, Bill has learned the vital truth that physical sports ability can be improved by applying the proper mental input; for physical output is forever linked to mental activity.

This book is about the mental side of sports and will lead most sports-minded people into a new dimension of excellence. It will open new avenues to success, for the mental game—properly applied—can achieve as much improvement as an equal amount of time spent on the practice field.

Here you can learn a formula that will allow people at all levels of sports activity to become better than ever before, to be able to break the barriers that kept them at a plateau of performance that they had thought to be permanent. But there is a price. Not a dollar price, but a price in time and self-discipline. If you can spend a minimum of twenty minutes a day, you can achieve exciting new heights of athletic success, so long as it falls within natural law.

Mental Dynamics techniques are not limited to psyching your opponent, or to event preparation, or to a single sport. Rather, they cover the entire range of sports activity and teach the reader to improve any, or all,

2   [1] Frank Litsky, *Superstars* (Secaucus, N.J.: Derbibooks, Inc., 1975).

parts of his game *permanently*. Beyond that, they also teach pain control, acceleration of natural healing, and many other benefits.

This book is not full of complicated theories or written in dull clinical terms that will boggle or stifle your mind. It is written in an easy-to-understand style, with emphasis on practical application, leaving the reader in control of his sports destiny. It is a success handbook for the casual and gifted athlete alike.

Success in sports is not a matter of chance. It is a matter of decision. It requires knowledge and commitment. Achievement in sports is not entirely a physical effort. It is also a mental activity, which at times exceeds physical activity in importance. All physical activity, regardless of its nature, is preceded by mental activity of some kind.

This book is designed to show you how to take the chance factor out of your pursuit of success in sports. It will provide you with the fundamental knowledge and mental conditioning techniques that can propel you to achievement beyond anything you may have dared to hope for. Those who train mentally with the same fervor used in physical training discover their athletic performance continually exceeding prior efforts, season after season.

Excelling in mental skills leads to excellence in physical skills. This book will introduce you to time-tested, athlete-tested principles and techniques that you can use to maximize your sports performance.

Examples of success, based on this book's techniques, abound. Take Geoff Wells, a young college pitcher who was so wild his coaches were about to give up on him until he discovered Mental Dynamics techniques. He began to use the book's relaxation exercises daily and was soon able to keep his pitches down consistently, and eventually developed exceptional control and total confidence. He was soon being evaluated by the Los Angeles Dodgers and California Angels.

A young high school jumper used these techniques to break his school record. A professional soccer coach was able to improve his communication with his players and enhance his ability to get the most out of each of them. He developed confidence and was able to avoid negation. Riley Moss, a mountain climber, was able to climb higher, bigger mountains by using the visualization exercises described in this book. And, like Bill Griffith, he was also able to keep his extremities warmer by programming his subconscious. He has since advanced to solo climbing.

Joann Zwingenberg, a figure skater, developed a new level of confidence and was able to make jumps and spins better than ever before, no longer afraid of the pain and embarrassment of falling. Perhaps more important, she applied these same principles to her social life with great success. This is a point worth making, for the techniques taught here, though groomed for the athlete, can be used anywhere in the broad stage of life.

A high school track coach had this to say about one of his star distance runners who had learned to apply Mental Dynamics techniques. "His daily workouts and weekend runs have been so good that I have had to give up running with him. He is breaking all the timed courses he has around town [and is] chopping whole minutes off his nine, ten, and eleven-mile courses." This young man had also developed confidence and greater insight into his running. He became a better team member and was later elected team captain.

And the list goes on. These techniques are the result of years of research and practical application. They are real—and they work!

This book presents a universal approach to the mental side of sports that can lead any dedicated athlete to success.

Here's a brief look at what you can expect to learn in subsequent chapters.

1. How to identify your weak spots and set up goals.
2. How to establish a plan of action designed to reach those goals.
3. How to program the plan of action into your subconscious mind.
4. How to develop a superb self-image.
5. How to develop concentration.
6. How to get motivated—and stay that way!
7. And much, much more!

This book can serve two purposes. It can make fascinating reading for the casual reader, or it can be used as a guidebook to significant athletic success. In the latter use it is important to read the book carefully *and follow instructions to the letter*. We assume in presenting this material that you are new to the concepts and principles of Mental Dynamics. Therefore, it is important that you read each chapter carefully, preferably more than once, and learn its message thoroughly before moving on to the next chapter. This is equally true for experienced athletes and beginners.

A superior athlete is a self-disciplined person. He masters the fundamentals of his sport before attempting more sophisticated levels of performance. This is just as true in mental training. Each step must be learned well in order to act as a springboard to the next step.

At the end of subsequent chapters you will find suggested mental projects which should be practiced for about a week. These little projects will allow you to explore the unlimited depths and power of your mind. They are harmless and fun and will illustrate some of the key points in this book.

Here are some additional suggestions for the serious student of Mental Dynamics.

1. Once you reach Chapter 4, spend a week practicing the principles learned in each chapter before moving on to the next chapter.
2. Keep a notebook. Jot down thoughts that are important to you. Write down concepts that you would like to memorize. Take notes that will help you to learn and remember. If you already have a training journal, include a section for your mental training records.
3. Learn each principle thoroughly. Become so involved with them that you will grow beyond intellectual awareness to the point where they become a part of your everyday life.
4. Practice daily!

Now then, are you ready to move on to new heights of athletic achievement? Then proceed to the next chapter, where you will examine the power of thought and learn what it can do for you.

2 Mind Over Body

You will begin to touch heaven, Jonathan, in the moment that you touch perfect speed. And that isn't flying a thousand miles an hour, or a million, or flying at the speed of light. Because any number is a limit, and perfection doesn't have limits. Perfect speed, my son, is being there.

RICHARD BACH[1]

The truly inner power necessary for athletic success is found in the fact that *Human beings are the product of their thoughts.*

This truth is so simple that it passes by most people. They never become truly aware of its deeper, hidden meanings. As you realize this truth and put it to work for you, it will change the course of your life in a way that is completely under your control. We will show you how to systematically practice that simple concept so that it will lead you to success in your sports activities.

Thousands of years ago Buddha recognized this truth when he said, "All that we are is the result of what we have thought, it is founded on our thoughts, and it is made up of our thoughts.[2] This is the same secret of success expressed countless times by other wise men. Ralph Waldo Emerson said, "A man is what he thinks about, all day long."

YOU BECOME WHAT YOU THINK YOU ARE

You are what you think you are; that is, you become what you think you are. You attract what you think and believe. Your life is a product of your thought and beliefs. Nothing in the world can change this fact. To realize your life as the fulfillment of your dreams, it is essential that your thinking always be in harmony with those dreams. Pascal said, "Thought constitutes the greatness in man."[3] Mind is the mighty mover.

[1]*Jonathan Livingston Seagull* (New York: Macmillan Publishing Co., Inc., 1970).

[2]U. S. Anderson, *Three Magic Words* (New York: Elsevier-Dutton Publishing Co., Inc., 1954).

[3]Ibid.

Conditioning your mind to the habit of successful thinking in your pursuit of athletic excellence is as essential as conditioning the body. For what can a superbly trained body accomplish if it is directed by a hesitant, uncertain mind that knows limitations, fear, and doubt, at both the unconscious and the conscious levels? A prime example occurred during the 1977 Wimbledon tennis championships. Chris Evert (later Chris Evert Lloyd), the acknowledged leader of the women tennis professionals, swept through the early rounds and looked unbeatable. The odds makers gave little hope to those who wished to bet against her. Yet, with barely a glimpse of her normal skill, Miss Evert fell victim to a lesser player. An affair of the heart, it was rumored. Just the kind of emotional trial that creates distraction, lack of concentration, lowered morale, and even self-doubt in all humans—even in the super athlete. Even one whose mind is well trained to have self-confidence and self-assurance can temporarily lose those qualities because of the thoughts associated with bad circumstances.

We are talking about the psychological law of cause and effect. Specifically, in sports, effect means athletic performance. Not only performance in competition but in all areas: training, practice, conditioning, sportsmanship, study perseverance, coachability, will, and pain tolerance, to mention but a few.

The law of cause and effect says that all effects have a cause and are a direct result of that cause. Thus, if the effect is negative or not in line with your goals, the cause is also negative. Conversely, if the effect is positive, the cause is positive.

The law of cause and effect further says that the first cause of all effect is thought. Thought is the first cause of how we experience ourselves and life. Thought precedes its expression whether in words, actions, or life-style. Nothing could be truer than the consistency of this relationship in the world of sports. Remember this, for it is the secret of your continual ability to improve and succeed:

What you think about becomes your reality!

What you think affects the outcome of every event. Even a team's collective thoughts affect the collective outcome of their efforts. Your thoughts affect your emotions. Your thoughts can cause indifference, discouragement, and a loss of confidence. Athletes can experience outright fear. On the other hand, your thoughts can give you confidence, hope, and determination.

You cannot think fearfully and build confidence. You cannot think doubtfully and build confidence. You cannot think of losing and expect to win. You cannot think indecisively and be quick to act. Nor can you think of failure and expect success. When you think doubt, you experience doubt. When you think rage, at officials perhaps, your body becomes rageful and less under your control.

A secret useful in all areas of life is learning to master thought. The secret in sports is defining your athletic goals and objectives and then keeping all thoughts aligned to those goals and learning to discipline your mind to oppose counteracting or wavering thoughts.

Since patterns of thought are often as habitual as behavior, the secret is to establish thought habits consistent with your goals. For instance, habitual thoughts of confidence, of enjoyment of your sport, of being a team player, of being a superb learner with ability and unlimited capacity, will lead toward success—if your goals are carefully defined. We'll talk more of goal definition later.

GET THE POSITIVE SELF-IMAGE HABIT

Self-image is another important factor in athletic success. While learning to master thoughts, it is essential to develop habitual positive self-image thoughts, for these, too, fall within the concept of cause and effect. Self-image psychology says, "How I think of myself will result in the way I will be, or perform." Self-image is our own concept of the kind of person we are. It has been built up from our beliefs about ourselves. Most of these beliefs, however, have been formed from past experience, our successes and failures, our humiliations and triumphs, and from the way other people have reacted to us. Once this self-image is formed, it becomes the habitual thought cause leading to a habitual effect, which is our behavior and performance. It is how we experience ourselves and life generally. Dr. Maxwell Maltz says, "All your actions, feelings, behavior, and even your abilities, are always consistent with this self-image."[4] In short, you will act like the sort of person you conceive yourself to be.

For example, there was the case of a football player who generally had a very positive self-image, except for one implanted shortcoming. Ever since childhood he had seen himself as Mr. Fumble Fingers. This led to fumbles at critical moments in several games. Despite all the ball-carrying drills set up by his coaches, his problem persisted. Finally, he recognized that fumbling was related to his self-image. He then began mentally to reprogram that part of his self-image. He learned to think of himself as sure-fingered, confident, and competent in the use of his hands. Soon thereafter his fumbling habit disappeared. This same principle can be applied to an endless list of problems in any sport . . . it has universal applicability.

Self-image psychology is not a new or theoretical concept. Rather, it is a principle learned from observations of human functioning. Those who think they can, can and usually do. Those who think they can't, usually don't.

[4]*Psycho-Cybernetics* (Englewood Cliffs, N.J.: Prentice-Hall, Inc., 1960).

Those who believe in themselves succeed and achieve. This principle has been emphasized for centuries and has been found in the writings of most major religions and philosophies of the world. "As a man thinketh in his heart, so he is." This familiar quotation is taken from Christian scriptures.

You are everything you have ever thought. Why is this so important to you as an athlete? As a person? Because each one of us—and that means you—can develop into anything within natural law when your self-image thoughts are of that kind of person. You can be, or become, do, or achieve, anything. You can develop and maximize your many talents if your self-image is of that sort of person and then, of course, merge that self-image with proper physical conditioning and knowledge of your sport.

Most people draw conclusions about themselves based on observation of their own past performance. They then conclude that that is how they are now, in the present. Many resign themselves and accept the idea that that is how they will be in the future. But how you will be in the future is greatly influenced by choosing to observe how you *want* to be in the future. You must see yourself as you wish to be, not as you were. Then through the mechanism of the mind, you grow into that image. Self-image can be changed! It is always changing. You can take charge of the change and mold it to support your goals. Let your goal reflect your self-image.

Unfortunately, most people have learned to live with the self-image they have developed from past experiences and associations. Friends and acquaintances tend to help us lock into existing ideas of what we are. "Josie *always* eats ice cream before going to bed," they say. Or "Bill will *never* do that!"

In the same way, actors are often typecast, finding it extremely difficult to get a variety of roles that truly reflect their range of talent. It's bad enough when others accept a preconceived idea of what we should be, but it is infinitely worse when we accept that limit and allow it to shape our self-image.

John L. Sullivan, the legendary heavyweight boxing champion, was a boisterous and prodigious drinker for much of his life. Yet he was able to break that image by a great exercise of will. He simply decided to go "dry" one day and never had another drink despite the protests of an alcoholic body. He was able to do that because he could visualize a self-image of himself as a nondrinker.

Similarly, you can overcome the influences of the past—influences that often keep people from developing a positive self-image for the future. Now you have the power to help yourself create a new self-image consistent with your future goals.

The important thing to realize is that the self-image thoughts come first, and in their marvelous, mysterious way they create reality of what you will be. Study this idea and learn it well. If you know what you want to become, begin by seeing yourself that way, regularly, continuously, unceasingly. That approach will lead to success.

This is a different idea. Most people will observe that some trait of theirs is less than perfect and will say, "Well, that's how I am." And they let it go at that. But you can now say, "Well, that's how I was," and then picture yourself as you choose to be and grow into that picture.

In subsequent chapters you will learn how to apply this principle to develop yourself mentally, physically, and in any other way you choose, to the optimum. You will learn to program your subconscious mind to achieve top performance, and then even extend the boundaries of the optimal.

AVOID THE IDEA OF LIMITATION

And now, for a moment, let's consider another word: *limitation.* Though our approach toward the goal of athletic performance and development is highly positive, limitation is a word all athletes striving for superior results need be aware of. The adversary to realizing your goals is not merely so much the opposing players as it is the long-held, hidden, insidious ideas and beliefs that inhibit the freest expression of latent physical talents.

For example, most track buffs are aware that the world record for the mile run is well under four minutes. Any runner of national or world stature realizes he must run the mile faster than four minutes if he has even a slight hope of competing successfully. A four-minute mile is rather commonplace today, yet only a few years ago it was believed that no one could ever do it. Why? Because everyone "knew" it was impossible. The athlete then knew the limits to which one could achieve. Any intelligent, rational human being knew that anything better was impossible. At least until Roger Bannister did it. He had to set new mental limits to make the breakthrough, proving the value of the proper self-image. With the walls of psychological limitations removed, the four-minute mile became common. You, as an athlete, can achieve anything within natural law. Natural law is not always known, but it is defined as far more limiting than it really may be.

If you have the courage to believe, and the will to pursue it further, learn to disregard, or reconsider, those things that you have been told or have come to believe can't be done. In this manner, you are free to set greater goals for yourself, many of which you will achieve.

A few years ago, a Mental Dynamics seminar student, a cyclist, was preparing for a training session at a nearby velodrome. He was asked how fast he should ride in order to break the track record.

"Oh, I couldn't do that," he replied. "I shouldn't even try."

"Why not?"

"I've always been taught not to peak out too early in the season."

The cyclist was obviously on another wave length at that moment. His comments were loaded with inferred limitations.

"You aren't expected to peak out now, just break the record," he was told. "After all, the record and peaking are not necessarily related. Don't let one thought limit the other."

Taking the advice literally, the cyclist went out and broke the record, and then progressed to peak at a new level later the same season.

Learn to monitor thoughts that suggest limitation. Remember, the ideas that you have regarding what is possible are based primarily on memories from the past—your own past as well as the past performance of others. We have already seen that the past does not always establish the proper criteria for future thoughts. Open your mind to new possibilities. Project your imagination one hundred, two hundred, or five hundred years ahead and visualize how athletes will be performing in your event then. They will have advanced because athletes along the way will break the binding beliefs that result in today's limitations. They not only will have practiced positive thinking but will have practiced *possibility* thinking!

They will have learned to believe that they can do anything, never questioning whether they could to it, only being concerned with how they would do it.

Before reading the next chapter, review the dreams and aspirations you have had in the past, for your life and in your sport. Identify the dreams, if any, that you may have ruled out or dismissed as too far out, impossible, or unrealistic. Take another look, reevaluate. Is it really so impossible? Suppose you could come close? Isn't that better than junking it altogether? Always remember Robert Browning's idea of reaching farther than your grasp. So much more is achieved that way. Think of the skills, abilities, and techniques that you would like to perfect. Realize that you can advance yourself confidently in any direction, once that direction is decided and you are committed to it. But if there is no direction, no dreams, no goal, nothing can be fulfilled. Remember these words of Henry David Thoreau:

> If one advances confidently in the direction of his dreams and endeavors to live the life he had imagined, he will meet with a success unexpected in common hours. He will put something behind and will pass an invisible boundary. New, universal and liberal laws will begin to establish themselves around and within him. And the old laws will be expanded and interpreted in his favor in a more liberal sense. And he will live with the license of a higher order of beings.

Before going forward you must know where you wish to go. *Put down some of your dreams and wishes on paper and we will refer to them in later chapters.* The next chapter will show you how your mind works and how it can be used as a tool to lead you to success.

In summary, remember these key ideas:

1. Human beings are the products of their thoughts.
2. What you think about becomes your reality.
3. Success as an athlete is not a matter of chance. It is a matter of decision, knowledge, and commitment. It is a mental activity, at times exceeding the physical in importance. All physical activity is preceded by mental activity.
4. Excelling in mental skills leads to excellence in physical skills.
5. The law of cause and effect says that how we live our lives is determined by thought.
6. Self-image thoughts determine how you perform as an athlete.
7. Thoughts of limitation produce limited results. Think beyond mental barriers.

3 Mind Zapping: A Twenty-Four Hour-a-Day Process

For they can conquer who believe they can.

VIRGIL[1]

Successful athletic performance is more mental than physical! Yet after hours of drilling, training, and conditioning it may be very hard to convince your body of this truth. But it is so, and athletes today are realizing and proving it to their own satisfaction. To say that athletics is a mental activity is one thing, but to really understand it is something else again. Coaches and athletes alike agree: "Yes, the mentals are really important," then mutter a few phrases like, "Positive mental attitude . . . PMA . . . motivation . . . think: win . . . think: positive." But beyond that, little attention is devoted to the subject, because the vast significance of the vital relationship between mind and body has not been fully appreciated or understood. The Eastern masters of such arts as kung-fu and karate come the closest to epitomizing this principle. Few other sports devote so much time and study to the whole-man principle of mind, soul, and body; and to the coordination of all three. Can you imagine yourself devoting as many hours to mental conditioning and training as you spend on the physical? When you thoroughly understand and appreciate the powers of the mind, and how to put thought to work for you, you will gladly schedule more time for mental conditioning and training.

Everything you do involves the use of your mind. The more completely you understand the basic simple functions of your mind, the more effectively you can use them in the development and performance of your athletic abilities. With proper mental conditioning and development, you will achieve greater mastery and control over your body. Not only the muscular skeleton system but every physical system of your body can be affected by your mind and thus by you, the potential master of your mind. When you learn to

[1] Herbert V. Prochnow and Herbert V. Prochnow, Jr., *The Public Speaker's Treasure Chest* (New York: Harper & Row, Publishers, Inc., 1964).

mentally control any of these systems, athletic performance can be enhanced in many subtle ways.

Canadian National Canoe Slalom Champ Bill Griffith can control the temperature of his hands. Paddling in cold, windy, crashing waters can freeze and stiffen the fingers, causing a considerable loss of the muscle control that is essential for intricate maneuvering through choppy waters and gates. Through mental mastery Griffith keeps his hands warm, without other aids, enabling him to guide his boat gracefully in and out of course gates.

The healing system of the body may also be influenced by mental effort. Many ills are brought on by misuse of the mind, and most of these can be prevented or corrected by proper mental techniques. You can also accelerate the healing of injuries, overcome jet lag, and adapt to climate or altitude changes. These are important factors for traveling athletes.

The mental aspect of athletics is more than PMA. It goes far beyond that, and those who study and practice diligently are ten steps ahead of their peers who do not.

To understand and use the methods of mental control (mentals) requires that you first learn basic principles of Mental Dynamics and conditioning. Once these are clear and acceptable to your intellect, the technique of mentally achieving your athletic goals will be easier to accept and practice. Your results will be far greater than the results achieved by those who practice mentals without this background.

The simplest approach to understanding this dynamic psychology is to understand the basic laws of suggestion and hypnosis. Now, we are not going to teach you hypnosis as it is generally understood by the public at large. You will not be mesmerized, nor will you learn how to hypnotize others. Rather, you will learn the psychological dynamics found in the phenomenon of hypnosis itself; and through this you will understand the principles of everyday psychology and mental programming. As you learn these basic dynamics of hypnosis, you will understand that they are present constantly, twenty-four hours a day. Thus, the title of this chapter: "Mind Zapping: A Twenty-Four-Hour-a-Day Process."

HYPNOSIS AND THE SUBCONSCIOUS MIND

Hypnosis is an important concept, and it is essential that you have a working definition of it and that you be aware of its implications in your own development. *Hypnosis is any situation or condition that permits thoughts or suggestions to be introduced to the subconscious mind.*

The subconscious mind is that part of your mind where all the action is taking place. It rules, governs, and oversees all bodily and behavioral functions. This is in contrast to the objective, or intellectual, mind with which we think, analyze, scheme, make decisions, and rationalize weaknesses. An example of our two minds at work is the person who in a fit or tantrum decides to hold his breath until he turns blue. His objective mind decides that the breathing function will stop, despite its harmful effects on the body. In a minute or two he will pass out from lack of oxygen, and his objective mind ceases to control his body. Immediately, the subconscious mind takes over its normal tasks of running the body's systems. No longer blocked out by the intellectual mind, the subconscious mind starts the body's breathing sequence, automatically trying to return everything to normal. In a few moments the conscious mind will awaken and will once again have the power to override the subconscious, if it wishes.

Unlike the conscious mind, the subconscious, by nature, is extremely literal. As a result, it functions to create realities from thoughts as it literally receives them. Let's repeat that because it's so important. *The subconscious is extremely literal and always functions to create realities from thoughts that have been presented to it.* Thus, when a goal is properly introduced to the subconscious mind, it will receive that goal-thought and—consistent with its literal understanding—work to create a reality from it.

When a thought is presented to the subconscious mind by yourself or by others, it is first processed by the thinking, reasoning, intellectual, conscious mind. If that thought does not appear logical or reasonable, the conscious mind may reject it and refuse it entry into the subconscious. Thus, in hypnosis the hypnotist looks for ways to immobilize the conscious mind or in some other way slip past the conscious screening activity and address suggestions directly to the subconscious mind. This is why the hypnotic subject can be convinced he is holding a chicken in his lap, when in fact no chicken is there. If a hypnotist induces a hypnotic trance such as we usually think of, he might touch your hand with a piece of chalk and suggest to you that he is burning your hand with a cigarette. Since your thinking mind is temporarily in a trance, and not functioning in its usual manner, the suggestion or thought would be received directly, uncritically, and literally by the subconscious mind, which would then proceed to create reality from it. You then experience the sensation or the realization of burning. If you are a very good subject, it may even produce a blister. The subconscious mind receives the thought without screening and strives to create reality from it. It does not actually produce burned cell tissue, but it will create a realization of burn, for it can create any realization possible within natural law.

In the preceding illustration, the thought could have been presented to your subconscious using any one of many possible mental conditions which we will discuss presently. It involved a condition, the trance, that permitted that thought to elude the critical evaluation of the intellect. In effect, the hypnotist acts as substitute for the subject's thinking, intellectual mind. While learning this definition of hypnosis, keep in mind that the subconscious mind is always literal. It receives thoughts literally and then creates realizations from them as it can. The subconscious mind always works this way, and properly programmed, it is the computer that will make you succeed. *Remember that*!

It is this principle that most psychologists have in mind when they note that we all have the ability to alter our lives by altering our attitudes of mind. And the attitudes of mind are basically the thoughts that we present to it.

With this definition of hypnosis, you will find the secret of successful realization of your goals and dreams. These principles are essential for you to know. By employing this definition you can effectively work with what is similar to self-hypnosis at any time for your improved self-image, self-confidence, or athletic performance.

CONDITIONS FOR PROGRAMMING THE SUBCONSCIOUS MIND

Hypnosis has been defined as any situation or condition that permits thoughts free access to the subconscious mind. Consider now five of the more common situations or conditions that may be used to create the hypnotic effect. In subsequent chapters you will learn techniques that employ some of these conditions, permitting you to intentionally program your subconscious mind in the furtherance of your athletic goals.

The first is the *deep*, or *sleeping*, *trance* state, a condition usually induced by a second party. It is the phenomenon that most people call hypnosis. It is, however, the least common hypnotic phenomenon of all, and it will not be used in this book. To all appearances, the subject, in a deep trance, has lost consciousness and control. The hypnotist is talking directly to the subconscious mind of the subject. The conscious, thinking mind has entered a hypnotic sleep state, or trance, and it cannot perform its usual analyzing, thinking, scrutinizing functions. The hypnotist, in effect, is substituting for the subject's conscious mind. The subconscious works creatively to bring forth a realization from the thought. Thus, when unrealistic suggestions are made—that the subject is a little puppy, for example, or is holding a hot potato—he will react as if it really is so. The subconscious causes the subject to realize these thoughts.

There is another trance state called the *waking trance*. It is a lighter trance, often induced by another person. Or, significantly, it may be brought on by oneself. Frequently, it occurs spontaneously, and it has been estimated that most people enter in and out of the waking trance as often as two or three hundred times a day. Sometimes this occurs for a split second and at other times it may last up to two or three hours. You may recognize it as the feeling that you experience when you are staring out of the window into space, or when you are driving and suddenly realize you don't remember the last few blocks. It is that same condition of concentrated attention that you experience when you are watching television intently, or when you are reading and are so deeply absorbed that sounds around you do not penetrate your concentration.

Most people are in a hypnoidal, trancelike state when they first awaken in the morning. This condition gradually leaves, though it may take fifteen minutes to four hours. This has been proven to be an excellent time to engage in mental programming activity, which is the systematic practice of providing your subconscious mind with your goal-thoughts. You will be given instructions for the use of this condition in Chapter 6.

The time just before drifting off to sleep is second only to the awakening period as a useful hypnoidal trancelike state.

The heavy and light trance states are most commonly thought of as hypnosis, but there are other conditions that also permit thoughts to be presented directly to the subconscious. One of these is *repetition*. A thought repeated often enough will eventually work its way past the conscious mind into the subconscious, which then acts literally to create reality from the thought. This is the principle behind propaganda efforts and advertising campaigns.

Advertisers use this principle most effectively by repeating messages through television, billboards, magazine ads, and other media. Continual, consistent repetition of a thought that suggests purchasing certain products has proven to be a viable technique in influencing people. Even Adolf Hitler expressed the view that if you repeat a lie often enough the masses will eventually believe it. Joseph Goebbels, Hitler's Minister for Public Enlightenment and Propaganda, administered the flagon of Nazi propaganda which so profoundly shaped events leading up to World War II. Cynically, Goebbels corrupted the principle discussed here. He wrote, "We are only helping the public when we call the imagination to our aid in certain cases where the record of facts is for some reason incomplete."[2]

Happily, this principle is well understood today and is therefore far less effective as a propaganda tool, but it still provides us with a proven tactic for developing positive changes in attitude.

You will notice by now a certain stress on the idea of getting thought past the conscious mind. This will be explained more fully later on, but for

[2] *Collier's Encyclopedia*, 1957, Vol. 9, p. 146.

now let us say that this is important because many athletic goal-thoughts might be resisted, doubted, modified, tampered with, or even rejected by your reasonable conscious mind. When the suggestion bypasses this scrutiny, the subconscious accepts it without scrutiny in its own literal way. And if humanly possible, and within natural law, it will seek to bring the suggestion to pass. For example, the goal of setting an endurance record might well be rejected by your intellect as being impossible for you and not your cup of tea. But the subconscious can take that suggestion and help you along as far as is possible within natural law.

Drilling in sports, running through a move, a play, or a technique over and over again is in effect utilizing this same principle. However, verbal or visual thought depicting these same aspects of your sport can also be used in a drill-like or repetitive manner for the accomplishment of many inner goals. It is a technique you will learn to use to supplement and enhance your regular physical drilling activity. And you will benefit from it!

The fourth factor used to introduce thoughts to the subconscious mind is *emotion*. When a strong emotion accompanies thought, fewer repetitions are necessary. Strong emotion attached to a single suggestion may be sufficient to cause that thought to project itself, unscreened, past the intellect and into the subconscious mind. It is as if emotion has given strong voltage—a charge—to the idea.

Thus, we easily remember an emotion-laden childhood experience that occurred only once. Such experiences were not only easy to remember but hard to forget. On the other hand, remembering such things as 7 × 9 = 63 was much more difficult because little emotion was attached. Repetition was required instead to implant that thought firmly in our subconscious.

The football coach's locker room pep talk is a prime example of the emotional appeal to the subconscious. Lesser teams have often won football games, against all logic, because of a superbly staged emotional speech by a coach or other team member. ("Win it for the Gipper!")

Mental relaxation is the fifth condition available for mentally programming your mind with long- and short-range athletic goals. In fact, mental relaxation is so effective and versatile that we usually suggest it as the method of choice—even over the trance state. Mental and physical relaxation usually go together and are used for many diverse purposes. Mental programming is only one of them, but it also serves mental and physical rest, recovery, re-energizing, and revitalizing, and even aids the management of pain and the acceleration of natural healing.

Mental relaxation differs from the trance in how it feels, because the individual retains full self-control and autonomy. With mental relaxation, you quiet the conscious mind and cause it to be inactive with respect to its functions of screening and evaluating. But you can always switch back anytime you wish.

In succeeding chapters you will learn techniques for achieving relaxation and you will become more proficient in the practice and uses of relaxation. Thoughts also can be effectively introduced to the subconscious mind during normal sleep. The subconscious mind never sleeps. Thus, when certain types of thoughts are properly introduced during sleep, they will be easily received and worked with by the subconscious.

INTRODUCE THOUGHTS
TO YOUR SUBCONSCIOUS MIND

In the chapters to follow you will learn several effective ways to introduce thoughts to your subconscious mind—thoughts slanted toward your athletic aspirations. However, if you are a good learner (a worthwhile goal in itself) and pay careful attention to all the ideas presented in this book, you will see how to apply this knowledge to other personal goals, in addition to becoming a superb athlete. You will be able to introduce thoughts to your subconscious that will lead to better feelings about yourself generally, to increase self-confidence, improve self-image in your personal life, work, or career. You will be able to present thoughts to your subconscious that will result in your becoming a more healthy, vigorous person. You will be able to program your mind for effective management of weight, eating habits, smoking, work and study habits, and self-discipline, to name but a few.

And so you will learn how to effectively create a mental state similar in effect to a hypnotic trance, but with complete self-control. You will be able to create a relaxed state of mind and then introduce your own thoughts and goals to your subconscious mind. You will be able to utilize the already existing mental programming conditions, such as the early morning trance, for good purposes. Sometimes you will accomplish it by repeating thoughts to yourself, employing the principle of repetition. If you wish, you may repeat those ideas with emotion, thereby providing them with greater power and impact. We will also teach you, in Chapter 11, how you can let your mind work with thoughts during the night while you sleep!

In short, by applying our definition of hypnosis, you can become a master of yourself, your life, and your sport. You will quickly and easily learn to create and utilize the programming factors effectively. You will learn how to introduce thoughts to your subconscious mind and then watch confidently for things to happen. Good things!

But remember, you really are in a hypnotic condition twenty-four hours a day. Keep this in mind and guard against negative thoughts. Choose your thoughts carefully. Let them always be consistent and in harmony with your goals. Like a gun: if you don't intend to use it, don't point it. In the same sense, never use thoughts with which you would not like to be hypnotized. Be selective.

In summary, remember the five conditions of hypnosis that allow direct entry to the subconscious. They are the deep trance, the light trance, repetition, emotion, and relaxation.

 **Relax Your Way to Success**

> People are always asking me what I think about when I'm
> running. The answer is nothing.
>
> O. J. SIMPSON[1]

Relaxation is the key to programming your mind to achieve athletic success.

Relaxation is an experience. The best definition of relaxation is attained by experiencing it, for it relates to a mental or physical state or condition that must be experienced to be known. It is a condition that, when understood and practiced, is of much benefit and satisfaction to the participant. In brief, we would propose to you that relaxation is one of the more perfect and natural states to which human beings can attain. It is a condition of mind or body that not only is natural but that probably reflects and represents one of the healthiest states you can achieve.

Relaxation is also an enabling condition. For when relaxed, physically or mentally, one is enabled to accomplish much that is not possible at other levels of functioning or consciousness.

As we consider relaxation, we will do so at both the mental and physical levels. Physical relaxation is essentially that which you recognize as a loosening of the muscles, the letting go and the freeing up. Creating a state, in effect, that is the opposite of tension. Physical relaxation can be accomplished throughout the body or in a single part of the body. One may relax the stomach only, or just a little finger. You may relax a specific part of your body for pain control or even for purposes of accelerating the natural healing process that goes on within.

MENTAL RELAXATION

Mental relaxation refers specifically to the relaxation of what we call the objective mind, sometimes referred to as the conscious or intellectual mind.

26   [1] Frank Litsky, *Superstars* (Secaucus, N.J.: Derbibooks, Inc., 1975).

This is the thinking, analyzing, criticizing, reasoning, classifying mind that we all know. It is also that part of our mind that says, "Yeah, but . . ." and thereby becomes an active resister of progress. When relaxed, this portion of our mind is slowed down. In meditative nomenclature it is expressed as "stilling the mind." One of the purposes of mental relaxation is to be still mentally. In meditation, for instance, when you decide to meditate, or have contact with God, or some other kind of spiritual experience, you first relax your intellectual mind.

We are concerned with the quieting of the objective mind, for it can be a vital stepping stone toward athletic mastery. With practice, you can easily quiet the machinery of the objective mind to the point that you have quiet awareness without much thinking about the things you are aware of. When that occurs, you might well ask, "What's left?" That's a good question. Pure consciousness is what's left. As you think, you have consciousness of what you are thinking. But when you stop thinking, you simply have consciousness of the remaining nothingness, which is often stillness.

When you have sensory input, you have consciousness of that which you can hear, see, taste, touch, and feel. When your thinking regarding those inputs ceases, you are left simply with pure consciousness. Attaining this state of pure consciousness can be a very special experience. It is the attainment of awareness; or consciousness of consciousness.

We have looked at mental relaxation from the vantage point of meditation. *Another important reason for learning the art of mental relaxation is to create a climate conducive to effective subconscious programming.* When you, the inner self, wish to program or reprogram ideas, data, or thoughts into your subconscious mind, it is important to create a mental condition that enables data to pass through or around that thinking, critical, objective mind. On occasion, the objective mind resists certain thoughts. For one reason or another it may have some difficulty with an idea that you wish to submit.

For example, a smoker with cigarette in hand, wanting to help himself stop smoking by changing his self-image to that of a nonsmoker, may find his intellectual mind quite resistive to the whole idea if it has not been stilled before submitting the idea to the subconscious mind.

The more we can relax the objective, intellectual mind, the easier it is to introduce thoughts and ideas to the subconscious mind, where it in turn works with it in its own creative way to achieve the results we want. Please remember this, for it is very important and will become more clear to you as you proceed through this book.

Another use of mental relaxation is maintenance and repair. Often, we exhaust ourselves during the day. We may not be doing a great deal of physical work, but mentally we may be extremely busy, and our mind grows tired just as our physical body does. It may be a day in which we make many decisions, deal with many problems, and worry about many things. We may be overanalyzing, overloading, and overworking the intellectual mind. Instead of relaxing and allowing things to flow along evenly and easily more of the time and letting the subconscious mind direct us, we tend to work our thinking mind too hard. As a result, we tend to become mentally fatigued.

Consider this generally accepted idea. By taking five-minute relaxation breaks two or three times a day, through lying back in a chair and relaxing—stilling your mind—you can get the equivalent benefit of one to three hours of sleep. After all, sleep is essentially a state of mental relaxation in which one permits the mind to relax. It also allows the subconscious mind to take over and sort out the day's inputs. It prepares you for the next thing to come. These little catnaps provide a "turning off" or a resting of the mental machinery. Thomas Edison used this technique throughout most of his adult life and was able to get by with a minimum of nighttime sleep as a result.

Mental relaxation is also an essential tool in the magnificent art of creative thinking and problem solving through the subconscious mind. In fact, in order to work effectively with the subconscious mind for any purpose at all—whether it be programming, personality development, meditation, creative thinking, problem solving, or anything else—it is essential that relaxation of the objective mind occurs first.

PHYSICAL RELAXATION

Now let us consider a few uses for relaxation of the physical body. The first use that we may make of relaxation in the body is also an aid in your mental programming. For instance, if you are working on a project such as visualization but are suffering from a headache or backache due to tension, you are likely to find mental visualization more difficult to practice. Programming and other mental activities are also tough to achieve when the body is uncomfortable. On the other hand, learning to relax your body to eliminate those tension-caused aches will help you to concentrate and achieve quicker and better mental activity.

Another use of physical relaxation is the maintenance and repair of the body, just as in mental maintenance and repair. There are several items that can be listed under this category. Healing is one. Healing in the body can be assisted by relaxation. There are many systems in the body, such as the cardiovascular and the digestive. But there is also a healing system. This is one of the most important systems in our whole life. During any given winter your own healing system may work to ward off the flu. Chances are very good that you will have a flu virus in your body, and yet your healing system will deal with it without your knowing about it. We are continually fighting off infection of some kind. It is now more commonly accepted in medical circles that many people even have cancer a number of times in their lives but never fully experience the symptoms because the healing system of the body has been fighting it and winning.

Another example of the healing system at work is in the mending of broken bones. We find that broken bones can be healed in a shorter time than previously thought as a result of proper mental and relaxation techniques. We know of a physician who had split his anklebone with an ax. This physician, very tuned in to the concepts discussed here, used various mental healing techniques that substantially accelerated the healing process. He was free of his crutches and out of his cast in just under three weeks. Normally, he would have required his patients to have taken six weeks, or more, for the same injury. It is a matter of mind over body. The mind can interrupt or otherwise affect any of the systems of the body. *Every system in your body can be touched and affected by your mind.* And relaxation is a prerequisite to using the mind for these purposes with maximum effectiveness.

You can see that relaxation is a vital ingredient for control of your mind and body. We will now begin to teach you a series of relaxation exercises that will give you that control. Please concentrate on these next few pages, because you are about to experience your first relaxation training exercise.

LEARNING RELAXATION

It is important to learn to relax your mind as well as your body, because relaxation can have a significant impact on your athletic performance. Witness the experience of famous tennis pro and sports researcher Vic Braden, as quoted in *Popular Mechanics Magazine*. "In our studies among hundreds of the students of the game [tennis]," says Braden, "I've found only one occasion where a significant improvement in play can be related to equipment. That's when you break your racket and have to borrow one. Quite often there's an immediate lift to your level of play; we attribute it to *relaxation*—the pressure's off, you can't be expected to perform well with a racket you're not used to, and so forth. We also find this lift lasts about as long as it takes you to go out and buy a racket just like the one you borrowed, then you're back to your old game again."

In the future, when we mention relaxation, we will refer not only to relaxation of physical tension but also to relaxation of the objective mind. *Mental relaxation is one of the conditions that also allow thought easy access into the subconscious mind*; and, as we mentioned in the last chapter, it is often the preferred method. So you will learn relaxation as part of the technique of mental programming, which we will detail in Chapter 6.

Relaxation is not the hypnotic trance; it is simply stillness, quiet, and peace. When you are mentally relaxed, you are awake and in control.

With this relaxation exercise you will learn to still and quiet your mind. First, you will learn a breathing exercise that will fill your lungs completely while you count mentally to four. Then you will hold your breath while counting mentally to two. Then you will sigh the breath out, after which you will pause for another two-count. Then you will repeat that cycle two or three times. This is designed to relieve you of surface tension. The next step is to involve the intellectual mind by doing some light breathing followed by counting down from seven to one. Each time that you count a number, you will visualize some color. When that phase has been completed, you will then learn progressive relaxation. This is an exercise in which you will have your first practical experience of talking to your subconscious mind in such a way that it will respond by causing your body to become very, very relaxed.

You will be the one in charge, however. We will simply lead you and show you what to do. When you have accomplished progressive relaxation, we will then offer a few positive thoughts for growth and instructions for returning to full alertness once again.

Relaxation Exercise for Chapter 4

Prepare yourself now to enter into your first beautiful relaxation experience. To begin, sit very comfortably in your chair, with both feet flat on the floor. Never do these exercises while lying down. You may fall asleep and the time will be lost. Adjust any tight or binding clothing and be sure that your hands are resting comfortably either on your lap or on the arms of your chair. Be certain that your hands are not in contact with each other. If it is comfortable for you, allow them to rest with the palms turned up, but if not, leave them in the position that is natural for you.

At this point you can decide between three different methods of using the following relaxation exercise. You can simply read it a few times until it is essentially memorized; you can have a friend read it to you; or you can record it on tape. Any of these methods will allow you to close your eyes so that you can become fully involved with the relaxation technique. However, the tape method will be the best method for most people, and additional information can be found in Chapter 11.

If you use a tape recorder or a friend, keep the voice even, using a monotone delivery. Introduce pauses where you see the periods (the number of periods indicates the length of the pause); this allows proper timing and gives your mind a chance to visualize completely the material being introduced to it. Do not struggle mentally to relax. Just listen to the voice and let relaxation occur naturally.

You will be using these same methods with the relaxation exercises in subsequent chapters as well, so it is important that you practice this first one very carefully and establish a positive learning pattern.

Record, memorize, or have read all the material between the rows of stars.

☆   ☆   ☆   ☆   ☆

We will begin with the breathing exercise. Close your eyes and follow this sequence. Count to four slowly, and during that four-count completely fill your lungs 1 . . . 2 . . . 3 . . . 4 . . . then hold your breath for two counts 1 . . . 2 . . . Following that, sigh the breath out, not holding back . . . . . . Sigh the breath out through your mouth and feel the pleasure of the exhalation. Feel the relaxing effect as you do it. One more time now, breathing in 1 . . . 2 . . . 3 . . . 4 . . . hold 1 . . . 2 . . . and just let it go . . . . . Breathe out all tensions, cares, and concerns, and feel the pleasurable effects of this exercise. Let your breathing return to normal as we prepare to quiet the mind and body even further.

Now take a very light breath, and as you sigh it out, think of the number 7 . . . Let your mind become very involved in thinking the number 7, and then to the very best of your ability, imagine the color red . . . Imagine the color red as you might find in a red apple or tomato. If you have any difficulty in visualizing colors or objects, do not be the least bit concerned about it. Just remember that however you do this exercise is the right way for now. Each time you do this you will improve and you will get better. With practice there is always improvement and perfection . . .

So now take another gentle sighing breath and as you let it out think the number 6 . . . and as you think the number 6, mentally picture the color orange to the very best of your ability. This might be helped by visualizing the fruit orange or the orange of a jack-o-lantern. Just mentally picture the color, and just think the color, and let the mind become very involved in what you are doing. Let your mind become quiet by these means. Don't analyze or anticipate. Don't question a thing. Just save your questions for later. But now, just for now, do it, enjoy it and feel how quiet, how still, how serene and tranquil the experience makes you . . .

Now with a very gentle sighing breath, think to yourself the number 5 . . . And while you are thinking the number 5, to the very best of your ability, visualize the color yellow; such as you might find in a big yellow grapefruit. . . . Visualize the color yellow, and then with another gentle sighing breath think the number 4 . . . Mentally think of the number 4 and visualize the color green. Green such as you would find in a deep, dark, rich green pepper. Visualize the color green as best you can. As you do so, allow your mind to become quiet and still. . . Quiet and still. . . The thinking mind is becoming so quiet, so peaceful. . . Turning all the time now into stillness. . . into the quietness within . . .

Let's take another gentle breath, and as you do so, think the number 3 . . . Visualize the color blue, such as the deep, rich blue sky in the summertime that we all love . . . Feel yourself sinking more gently . . . more quietly into relaxation . . . And now, another easy breath. Sigh it out and think to yourself the number 2 . . . Mentally picture the color purple, such as in a purple grape, and let your mind become even more quiet and still . . . Now take a final gentle breath and think the number 1 . . . Visualize the color violet and allow yourself perfect peace and stillness . . .

At this point you are enjoying a new degree of relaxation. You have done well, and will continue to reach new levels of relaxation. Each successive time you will continue to progress and improve in your ability to relax yourself.

Now let's go on to the next phase of relaxation, that which we call progressive relaxation. So just tell yourself that it will be very easy to do. Tell yourself that as you do this, if there are any sounds that are not a part of what we are doing, these sounds will act as a trigger mechanism, causing you to relax even more deeply. Tell yourself this and give yourself that thought. Those sounds may simply blend into your thoughts and not even be heard. The only exception to this is if there are any sounds of an emergency nature, requiring your attention, in which case you will be easily able to arise from the exercise and take care of the problem.

Now go on to progressive relaxation in the following manner. Simply place your awareness on the different parts of your body and then mentally speak to them . . . tell them to be relaxed, but do nothing else. The relaxation will follow of its own accord.

And so to begin, direct your awareness to the top of your head and become aware of the skin stretched across the skull, be aware of the scalp from hairline on back, and from ear to ear . . . Speak to your scalp and tell it to be relaxed, be loose, be free, be still and let go . . . . . Having done that, allow your awareness to slide down to your eyes and be aware of the muscles around them, over and under and around the eyes, and tell them to be relaxed . . . Speak to them in your mind and tell them to let go. And as the muscles of the eyes relax, you will find the entire body relaxing faster because the body relaxes as the little muscle of the eyes relax. Next, let your awareness drift around the facial muscles. Drop your awareness from the eyes down past the nose to the mouth and the chin. Let your awareness flow in a line from the chin back to the ears and the jaw muscles in front of the ears. Be aware of the cheeks and all the flesh of the face, and tell it to be relaxed . . . . completely. And now, as you continue, let your awareness drift on to the mouth and your tongue. Be aware of the tongue in your mouth from tip to stem, from side to side, and tell the tongue muscles to relax, be still and let go.

You will begin to notice that as the muscles of the tongue relax you will find that the mind—your objective mind—is even more still. It is as if the machinery, the cogs of the mind, have been coming to a standstill and are now stopping. So let your awareness drift down to the shoulders on both sides, in front and in the back ... Let your awareness slide down both arms, through the muscles of both upper arms, past the elbows and down to the lower arms ..... Down the wrists into both hands ..... Speak to them. Tell them to relax, be loose, be calm. Now let your awareness drift back to your chest .... Tell those muscles to relax. You will soon notice that as the chest relaxes, your breathing will become easier and easier.

Let your awareness slide down to your abdomen, where you can tell the muscles of the upper and lower abdomen to relax in turn. Feel that wonderful sense of peace and tranquillity that envelops you ....

Finally, let your awareness travel to your thighs, knees, calves, ankles, and feet. Right down to the toes of both feet. Speak to them and tell them all to relax, be loose, be free, be still, and let go .... Now feel how wonderful it is to be completely relaxed ......

Make a mental note that it is you who has done the job. *You* have relaxed yourself. *You* are the one who has been speaking to your own subconscious mind. *You* are the one who has been giving orders to your subconscious mind, making it work for you, helping you to become a relaxed person mentally and physically ....

In the future, you will be able to become even more relaxed than you are now. Notice how much more you are relaxed after this exercise than when you first started .... Notice that you have virtually no sense of body feeling because relaxed muscles do not send messages to the brain .... Now is the time for your subconscious mind to receive any positive thoughts for health and welfare. Thoughts in accord with your wishes ... So, as you enjoy your relaxation, you now know that you have already begun your training to be a good student of relaxation. You are a good student of mental programming ... As you sit here now, relaxed and quiet, continue to let your mind flow free as you consider these positive thoughts for growth and development.

You have learned that you are what you think you are. That your life is a product of your thoughts and beliefs ... And so you resolve here and now to master the fine art of keeping all your thoughts in line, under control. Resolve that they will always be in complete harmony with your dreams and goals. In the days to follow, practice correcting any thoughts that are not 100 percent in harmony with your athletic or other goals. If you detect thoughts of doubt, make your thoughts ones of confidence. If you hear "I can't," change it to "I can." . . . . . If you think "It's hard," change it to "It's getting easier." . . . . . Make all your thoughts the thoughts of a superb, excelling athlete . . . . As you choose to be a success in sports, you will also choose to think success thoughts. *You will practice success thinking until it is automatic* . . . . . As you choose to be a confident athlete, practice confident thinking . . . . If you are uncertain how to think in a confident way, then associate yourself with confident people. Listen to their confident style of thinking and speaking . . . . What you think about becomes your reality . . . . What you think affects the outcome. So practice thinking confidently. Be like the kind of person you dream of becoming. Spend some time defining this dream because you'll need that definition later in the next chapter . . . . .

From now on, as you exercise new patterns of thinking, be sure to also practice eliminating ideas of limitation from your speech . . . . Learn to think that within natural law anything is possible once you have learned how. Learn never to question *whether* something can be done, rather ask *how* can it be done . . . . As you assume this attitude, you will succeed at far more than ever before because you will be free to try more than ever before. You may not succeed at everything, but you will have more frequent and dramatic successes than ever before. Free up your thinking to unlimited possibilities . . . . .

With these thoughts presented to your subconscious, it is time to return to full alertness once again. You are going to count back up from 1 to 7. With your eyes closed, tell yourself that each number brings you at least one seventh of the way to full alertness. When you arrive at 7 with the eyes still closed, take three deep breaths, and on the peak of intake of the third breath, then—and only then—open your eyes, smile, stretch, feel alive and alert. You will be refreshed and revitalized and in tune with life and ready to go on with the next thing on your schedule.

☆   ☆   ☆   ☆   ☆

Advanced relaxation techniques will be introduced at the end of subsequent chapters. There, you will learn how to apply relaxation to the specific principle of Mental Dynamics being discussed in that chapter. To get maximum benefit from the advanced relaxation exercises, you should first practice what you have learned in this chapter for a week. In that way the principle of repetition will help to make relaxation a regular and natural part of your life, and will enhance your ability to make Mental Dynamics work for you.

Mental Project for Chapter 4

Three terms of importance to students of mental programming, suggestion, and hypnosis are *ideosensory, ideomotor,* and *ideoaffective.* This means simply that the idea of a sensory, motor, or affective experience gives rise to that experience. If one holds the idea of a taste, sound, or smell in consciousness, one is most likely to experience that taste, sound, or smell. On the other hand, before motor activity such as standing up, walking, or running will occur, the idea must have entered the mind. Finally, when the idea of an emotion is entertained, it will most likely cause that feeling to be experienced.

To experience this principle is more convincing than simply to read it. Therefore, follow these steps and see how you experience it. Then we will discuss application.

EXERCISE: Sit down, as in preparation for relaxation, close your eyes, and let your body and mind be still. Relax yourself physically and mentally for just a few moments.

When this has been accomplished, imagine a bowl of fruit on a table. Imagine any fruits you wish but include a lemon. Proceed to examine each fruit in order. One at a time, observe their colors, patterns, texture, and weight. Finally, take the lemon and examine it. Look it over carefully. Notice its coloring, shininess, moisture, and shape in detail.

Now cut the lemon into slices and observe the cross section in detail. Finally, take a slice of lemon and bite into it or put it in your mouth.

Now without any further instructions you are probably already experiencing everything from pucker to sour taste to salivation. For many of you, reading this has already triggered that reaction.

This is a simple demonstration of how the ideosensory action occurs. It demonstrates clearly how the mind tends to create a realization from thought.

You may continue this experiment by applying the ideoaffective principle.

Again—in this relaxed state of mind—take a few moments to recall some event (the more recent the better) in which you experienced a high degree of embarrassment. What was your most embarrassing moment? Think of it. Imagine it. Relive it in your mind now. Visualize every detail. The further you carry this, the more likely it is that you are beginning to feel or experience that embarrassment.

Sometimes when this principle is demonstrated in groups, some participants actually blush or get sweaty.

CONCLUSION: The subconscious mind does not really distinguish between actual and imagined experiences.

APPLICATION: Imagine getting hot under the collar from bad officiating versus imagining staying calm, cool, collected, and unaffected, your performance only improving. You can imagine the feeling of confidence, poise, and knowing until that feeling actually comes to you; a feeling most important in your athletic performance.

You can (and do) create virtually any feeling at all. Helpful or not. Through practice, you can choose the feelings you want.

5 Be a Winner – Set Goals

Far better it is to dare mighty things, to win glorious triumphs, even though checkered by failure than to take rank with these poor spirits who neither enjoy much nor suffer much, because they live in the gray twilight that knows not victory nor defeat.

THEODORE ROOSEVELT[1]

Winning in sports may be the most important goal of all. But do not let winning mean only a competitive victory over the other person or team. Rather, let it be a personal thing—a victory, as it were, over yourself. Let winning mean successfully achieving goals of mastery over your mind, emotions, and body—a mastery so great that you are able to perform perfectly in athletics in every respect.

Winning in sports means setting and achieving many personal goals. Winning is also the further development of your character. It is the successful development and mastery of virtually every aspect of your being. To the degree that you have mastered your emotions and have trained your body; and to the extent that you have acquired mastery of your mind and learned to maintain desire and motivation, and have mastered concentration and determination; to the extent that you have accomplished these and countless other skills and traits, to that degree you are a winner. In balance, to the degree that you have advanced beyond your opponents in the mastery of these factors, you will prevail in competition.

Remember, outward victory in competition will always be the result of inwardly being a winner. Competitive victory is the logical end result of successfully achieving other goals and need not be the primary goal itself. It is a result. Winning can be defined as progress toward, and achievement of, a worthwhile goal. To be a winner, therefore, demands that you set goals, including the goal of believing yourself to be a winner. It includes a winner's self-image.

In order to sharpen motivation, it is essential that your goals be determined. *For goals provide the reason and incentive that cause and sustain*

[1]Caroline Thomas Harnsberger, *Treasury of Presidential Quotations* (Chicago, IL: Follett Publishing Company, 1964). Used by permission of Follett Publishing Company.

your activity. Goals provide stimulation. They provide the positive reasons for doing something when contrary reasons appear. Goals keep the athlete going when pain, frustration, and even boredom of training say, "What's the point of it all? Why bother?" Goals provide renewed hope when disappointment and setbacks occur.

Success in any area of life is possible only by setting achievable goals. "Achievable goals" is an important phrase and deserves some further explanation. Care must be taken to avoid setting too large a goal as an initial step. Its very enormity—especially to an inexperienced goal setter—can discourage belief. Therefore, break large desires into small pieces; design a path to the large goal that includes several milestones along the way. Let each milestone be a goal to be conquered in turn. Its achievement will build your self-confidence and make the next step a little easier until the final, large goal no longer looks like the impossible dream, but simply another stepping stone.

We judge success as being progress toward a major goal, and the intermediate goals become a measure of progress. As an athlete you can realize personal achievement and success beyond your present attainment by setting goals, by *committing* yourself to them and then moving toward their accomplishment.

Winning in sports may not always be found in beating the competition or being first. Rather, it can also be found in the achievement or the progress toward realization of your goals. Though victory in competition is fun, it need not be the only goal nor the most important one, especially for the amateur athlete. Actually, it is more realistic for you to become the very best possible athlete that you can become. Everyone cannot always be the victor over everyone else. But everyone can become his own best athlete and can have victory over himself. *Losing to another is not failure, but failing yourself is losing!*

STEPS TOWARD SUCCESSFUL GOAL SETTING

To be a *consistent* winner requires that goals be *consistently* set. Setting goals involves seven steps: (1) survey yourself—know where you are right now with respect to your development, aspirations, and dreams; (2) choose goals that are based on that survey and put them in writing; (3) carefully, and completely, define your goals in writing; (4) develop and write down your plan of action; (5) commit yourself to their attainment; (6) develop feelings of enthusiasm, dedication, and excitement for your goals; (7) present your goals to your subconscious mind. Now let's look at these steps in more detail.

STEP 1: EVALUATE YOUR PRESENT STATUS. Take from fifteen minutes to an hour, by yourself, away from distractions, to reflect on your present state of athletic development. Let this reflection be broad in scope. Rate yourself on paper in as many categories of your athletic activity as you can. As you list different factors, rate them on a scale from 10 to 1, with 10 signifying optimal development.

In what areas should an athlete rate himself? The list is endless, since each athlete has his or her own special needs and desires, unique to the individual as a person and as an athlete. In addition, there are many areas of concern to be considered that are common to all athletes. These can be divided into two broad categories: internal and external.

Rate yourself, for example, in the following areas of internal concern or interest: confidence . . . coachability . . . courage . . . adaptability . . . playing under pressure . . . pain tolerance . . . concentration . . . sportsmanship . . . emotional control . . . aggressiveness . . . leadership . . . determination . . . ability to take criticism or suggestions . . . patience . . . ability to relax . . . respect for others . . . self-image . . . decision-making ability . . . imagination . . . sense of humor. The list could go on, but these are a good representative sample.

Maximum mastery in any one of these areas would significantly affect your athletic performance. Mastery in several or all of them would lead to outstanding performance when accompanied with proper physical training.

Now rate yourself in these areas relating to the exterior or physical functions of your sport: speed of bodily actions and reactions . . . breath control . . . physical techniques, of which you can list dozens, depending on your sport . . . agility . . . grace . . . adeptness . . . balance . . . energy recovery . . . eye-hand coordination . . . timing . . . physical endurance and consistency. When you are able to rate yourself 9 or 10 in most of these areas, you will be an outstanding athlete.

When making this personal survey, it may be helpful to use the Mental Dynamics Suggested Goals List in the Appendix for reference. This list includes important qualities and skills desirable for developing into an outstanding performer. Run through the list of items and rate yourself on those that are appropriate to you and your sport. Feel free to add other items that you think apply.

If you decide that you cannot be sufficiently objective when rating yourself, ask some friends, co-players, or your coach to give their evaluation on the 10-to-1 scale. Before doing this, be sure that you can honestly rate yourself 8, 9, or 10 in your ability to accept criticism or evaluations from others.

Now, to illustrate what we've been telling you, let's look at a young married couple, Joe and Jenny Athlete. Joe is a professional baseball player, an outfielder for a Triple-A farm club. His desire is to make the jump to the big leagues, so we can see that his goals will be career-oriented. Jenny, on the other hand, wishes to develop her tennis skills for recreational purposes. She took up the game to help keep her busy while Joe is on the road with his team.

Joe hits the ball for a good average (.330), but he lacks power. He is a good fielder and has great speed. He realizes that his mental attitude is sometimes poor and he tends to have a quick temper.

Jenny has passed the beginner stage, but continued play doesn't seem to help her to improve her results. She loses more than she wins but always maintains an even composure and is a popular playing partner.

Joe and Jenny buy a copy of this book and agree to help one another apply it to satisfy their individual athletic ambitions. They filled out a survey form using selected goals from the list in the Appendix, plus a few of their own. Here's the way the surveys looked after a careful analysis.

	JOE'S RATING	JENNY'S RATING
Mental		
Superb self-confidence	8	5
Powerful concentration	8	6
Ability to relax	6	8
Accept constructive criticism	7	8
Relax with "away" fans	6	—
Emotional self-control	5	9
Great determination	9	5
Avoid being "psyched out"	5	5
General		
Good self-image as an athlete	8	4
Good self-image as a person	7	9
Master all official rules	9	7
Be a good learner	8	8
Environmental adaptability	7	6
Good sportsmanship	7	10
Team		
Rapport with teammates	8	—
Ability to accept authority	7	—
Inspire team loyalty	5	—
Ability		
Better ground stroke control	—	5
Ability to steal more bases	5	—
Improved volleying	—	4
Better bat control	5	—
Higher batting average	7	—
Quick reactions	9	7

	JOE'S RATING	JENNY'S RATING
Conditioning		
To enjoy practice	8	4
To give maximum effort	10	8
Great endurance	9	6
Practice Mental Dynamics	4	3

STEP 2: GOAL SETTING. This is easier now that the survey has been completed. Simply review your survey form and check each item rated 5 or less. Those items will most likely lead to choosing a goal. For instance, if you rate your ability to concentrate as a 4, then set a goal of becoming a master of concentration. If your decision-making ability is rated as 5, then set a goal to always make the right decision at the right time. If you have many items rated 5 or less, work with them before going on with the 6 or over group. If there are only a few items rated 5 and under, proceed with perfecting those items along with others rated higher on the scale. You will no doubt decide to *prioritize your list of goals if there are many to begin with.*

Joe Athlete chose the following goals from his survey list. He decided to improve his emotional self-control; to avoid being "psyched out"; to inspire team loyalty; to improve his ability to steal more bases; to develop better bat control; and most of all, to consistently practice his Mental Dynamics.

Jenny's ratings were generally lower than Joe's, so she had a few more initial goals. They included: developing more self-confidence; establishing great determination; avoiding being "psyched out"; creating a good self-image as an athlete; learning game strategy; developing better ground stroke control; improved volleying; learning to enjoy practice; and like Joe, consistently spending time on Mental Dynamics.

One method for setting goals, then, is to survey where you are now, in all areas of your athletic development. When you identify areas in which you wish to improve, they will become your goals. *Put your goals in writing* so they can be checked regularly to allow evaluation of your progress.

If you participate with a team, the same procedure can be followed by the team as a unit. Together, develop team goals that become each individual player's goals, in addition to the player's personal goals. Be sure each team member has the goal that he "is a superb team member and enjoys fantastic team spirit and unity."

Finally, consider long-range as well as short-range goals. How do you wish to see yourself a year from now? Five years from now? Where will your

42   progress take you? Do you envision yourself coaching or teaching someday?

What kind of overall record do you intend to establish? Do you intend to remain an amateur? Will you retire or turn professional? For long-range goals you must think ahead.

STEP 3: DEFINE YOUR GOALS AND PUT THE DEFINITIONS INTO WRITING. This is important for several reasons. First, it ensures greater clarity. People usually assume they know what they mean when they declare their intentions. But, in fact, they are often very vague. Words are used, but those using them often do not have specific or conscious meaning for the words. This is extremely important because you cannot achieve a goal any better than you have defined it. You cannot succeed with a goal in excess of your understanding of it or in excess of the meaning that you have for it.

One young runner we know has said, "My goal is to be a great runner." Sounds reasonable enough. But he must answer the question "How great? How great is great?" Is he to be a big runner locally, or in his hometown, regionally, nationally, or internationally? What does being a great runner mean in terms of speed, time, or distance? What kind of runner: sprinter or long-distance? Or perhaps a miler, cross-country, or marathon. That young man has more defining to do. He must be clear about what he intends before he can effectively achieve his goal.

Another athlete may declare a goal of having a winning season. But what does that mean? A 51 percent winning record? A 60 percent winning record? To become eligible for the play-offs? He, and you, must define the exact meaning of the words. It is not uncommon for people to falter when pressed to explain real meanings. For example, developing concentration is an important goal for an athlete. However, it is a word that many athletes have trouble explaining and it is something they have trouble doing. Define the term as you mean it. Can you tell someone else, clearly, concisely, and in detail what concentration means to you? Try it . . . you may be surprised.

The goal must be defined so that your subconscious mind can know what you intend. Because shortly you will learn to intentionally present your defined goals to your subconscious mind. It in turn will help you achieve the goals. But remember, your subconscious mind works with your goal only as well as you have defined it. Remember, too, that the subconscious mind is very literal and works best with sharp inputs. It cannot work with gray areas and sloppy thinking. *If you are vague in your definition, your subconscious will be vague in its understanding, AND IN ITS EXECUTION!*

Finally, by putting your goals and definitions on paper, you are already in the process of programming them. You are taking the first step toward their realization. This procedure will also help you to keep them permanently in mind, so you will stick with them until you establish a rating of 9 or 10 on your rating scale.

Take each goal and write out a complete and concise definition. In some cases you may require a full page per goal, but more often a shorter definition will do the job. Where team goals are involved, it is effective for the team as a group to follow the same procedure and to carefully define just what is meant by their goals.[2]

To get an even better idea of defining goals, let's take a look at the way Joe defined one of his:

> My goal is to develop *better bat control*. I want to be able to consistently hit to the right side on hit and run plays. I want to be able to consistently hit down the line on inside pitches because I'm basically a line-drive hitter and that will give me more extra-base hits. I will also improve my bunting ability, both for sacrifices and for base hits. I will learn to "lay off" of bad pitches. Through these techniques I will raise my minor league batting average twenty points to .350 by the end of the season.

STEP 4: DEVELOP AND WRITE DOWN A PLAN OF ACTION. This step is easy to follow and will help you meet your goals. Writing your plan of action reinforces the goal you have in mind. It helps to clarify the goal and provides more positive working materials for the subconscious. The procedure is simple. Review your list of defined goals, then reflect on the steps, actions, routines, and schedules necessary to implement that goal.

In some cases, mental programming techniques alone may be sufficient, requiring no special plan of action. For instance, the goal of becoming more decisive calls for a thorough definition of a decisive player. But to achieve this goal would require only the use of mental programming as taught in Chapter 6. Beyond that, a plan of action may not be necessary.

On the other hand, if the goal is to thoroughly know the strengths and weaknesses of an opposing player or team, you would need to develop a plan or strategy for research. Where will you find the desired information? How will you obtain it? How will you put the data into an effective plan of action? In this case, you will want a plan that supports the programming of the goal of having outstanding knowledge of the opposition. Write out your plan of action and, when appropriate, include *time lines* and *target dates*. These will help you to keep progressing along the way and they will help you gauge your progress.

As an example, here's the way Joe set up his plan of action designed to develop better bat control.

---

[2] See Appendix for Starter Sheet for Defining Goals. This will help you get started with your goal definitions.

My plan of action for my goal of achieving better bat control is:
1. I will immediately start "choking" my bat.
2. I will immediately start practicing a shorter backswing in my batting stance. In two weeks I will use it in league games.
3. I will schedule thirty minutes of extra batting practice every day, and split the time evenly between hit and run plays, pulling inside pitches and bunting. I will swing at good pitches only!
4. After two weeks I will start bunting for hits in league play.
5. I will spend twenty minutes a day mentally programming my subconscious to help me realize this goal.

STEP 5: COMMIT YOURSELF TO THE SUCCESSFUL ACHIEVEMENT OF YOUR GOALS. This is essential for those who lack enough commitment to their goals and are easily stopped in their tracks. These people can usually be talked out of continuing by any number of negative forces.

We have suggested commitment, as a fifth step, rather than an earlier one because after doing your survey, and setting goals, defining them, and plotting out a plan of action, you have been led into greater familiarization and stimulation with your goals. In other words, as you follow steps 1 through 4, you develop that commitment to follow your goal through to the end. The task becomes a known quantity, something you can attack in concrete steps, rather than a nebulous thought without boundaries. You have already committed yourself through doing the first four steps.

Commitment is vital. It is a pledge to yourself that your goal will be achieved. Nothing can stop you. Be determined! *Remember, your overall goal is to be a consistent winner.* Sticking with each goal until it is realized is the hallmark of a winner. Success is achieving your goal. As you commit yourself to these achievements, and succeed with them, you will experience a feeling of *pride, satisfaction, and the thrill that comes with victory.* You will be enjoying many victories within yourself as well as in the arena of sports competition.

WINNERS NEVER QUIT, AND QUITTERS NEVER WIN!

STEP 6: DEVELOP STRONG FEELINGS ABOUT YOUR GOAL. The subconscious, which leads you to the attainment of your goal, is especially responsive to *feeling.* Therefore, wherever possible, generate as much feeling for your goals as you can. Emotion, as you will recall from Chapter 3, is one of several conditions that help thought and suggestion, including your goals, into the subconscious mind. Emotions provide the added voltage and power that propel your goal-thoughts deeper into the subconscious mind. Desire, wanting, and enthusiasm are very important feelings! These are the emotions that provide the energy and force that are more than just knowing. Emotion is the power that impels us to our greatest achievements. It is also the power that leads some to great folly if negatively applied. Strive to muster as much positive feeling and desire for each goal as you possibly can. Want it . . . desire it . . . let nothing—and no one—deny you!

Company sales meetings are a good example of the value of emotion in goal achievement. Many are like college pep squads at work prior to the big homecoming game. The meetings often include songs, slogans shouted in chorus, and inspired speeches by sales managers. Tom Watson, of IBM, was one of the masters of this method. He would send his dark-suited salesmen running from meetings literally panting to find a customer . . . and another customer . . . and another, until goals were met and surpassed. One need only look at the success of IBM to see how well the system works.

It is harder to summon positive desire and emotion for some goals, and we don't all have a Tom Watson to light our fire. Some aspects of physical training, conditioning, or drilling, though essential to good performance, may seem boring and even unpleasant. But there is a way around that problem. Here are two suggestions that should help you build enthusiasm and desire even for dull tasks.

1. Revise the goal slightly to include the thought that you will *enjoy* regular, vigorous, prescribed training. If you are going to pursue any goal, you may as well include enjoyment as part of it. You'll do a better job.
2. Reflect on the rewards of having your goal achieved. For instance, if you have defined a goal of physical training that includes weight lifting or extensive calisthenics, but have little enthusiasm for such efforts, think of the results you will achieve instead. Look at the benefits and rewards that will accrue as you achieve that basic training goal. See yourself enjoying the end results, the pride, the satisfaction, the reactions of your peers. Hold that carrot in front of you. Such reflections will help you muster more enthusiasm.

STEP 7: PRESENT YOUR GOAL TO YOUR SUBCONSCIOUS. This is a complete procedure with several steps which will be discussed in the next chapter.

Before proceeding to the next chapter on mental programming techniques, be certain that you are properly prepared for it. Review the first five chapters to be sure—absolutely certain—that you understand all the principles taught so far. Failure to study and review may result in your feeling confused as you study forthcoming chapters. Be sure you have followed steps 1 through 6 in this chapter on goal setting. They are:

1. Survey your present situation.
2. Review the survey and list your chosen goals in writing.

3. Define your goals in detail, and write them down.
4. Write out a plan of action for each goal.
5. Commit yourself to the attainment of your goals.
6. Summon positive feelings toward your goals.

As you follow these steps carefully, you will walk the same path as have the few truly successful people in the world. Learn these steps well. Practice them. Drill with them as you would drill in your sport, until they are second nature to you. In so doing, you are well on your way to becoming a winner!

Relaxation Exercise for Chapter 5

This is your second relaxation exercise. For best results, prepare for this exercise in three ways.

First, recall from the past week one of your most successful and pleasant relaxation experiences. Remember one in particular, as you will be visualizing it very soon.

Second, mentally design some passive scene of nature, something in the wilderness perhaps, in a valley, on a mountain, or on the seashore: some place you love very much, some place where you can relax and enjoy yourself completely, a place that you can easily visualize. If you know of no such place, make one up before beginning this exercise.

The third step is to bring to mind some of your athletic dreams and goals. In Chapters 4 and 5 you were asked to think of them and write them down. Now you will use them as part of this exercise so that you can go beyond relaxation into visualization of your goals. Therefore, refresh your memory and proceed. If necessary, refer to your written material.

To achieve relaxation more quickly, simply close your eyes and follow the same procedure you used in Chapter 4.

☆ ☆ ☆ ☆ ☆

Get into the comfortable position you've adopted, and then begin with the breathing exercise which relieves surface tension. Breathe in for a count of four, hold your breath for a count of two, and then sigh your breath out. Let the counts be roughly equivalent to a pulsebeat, and breathe out all tensions and concerns. Do this three times.

Now let your breathing return to normal and then move on to the next stage of relaxing both mind and body. Recall your best relaxation experience of the past week. Recall the level of relaxation that you achieved and enjoyed the most. Remember how the hands and the fingers felt and the feet and the toes. How loose and limp they were. . . . In your mind imagine them feeling that way right now.... And then remember how the arms felt. The lower and upper arms.... How completely loose and limp and relaxed those muscles were. And now imagine them feeling that way again .... And the same with the shoulders in front and back.... And the chest muscles. Just remember how completely relaxed your body had become..... and imagine feeling that way now. Recall how loose and free the muscles of the upper and lower abdomen has become, and feel that way now .... The same with the legs, the thighs, and the calves. .... Remember how totally relaxed they were. And remember the back muscles and how the back of the neck felt. All the way from the back of the skull, right down through the shoulders and into the back..... Recall the upper and lower back muscles and how relaxed they were. Imagine them feeling that way right now.... In your mind recall how still you had been, remember how quiet and at peace you had become. Imagine your mind now being that relaxed, completely still......

And now you're going to count down from 7 to 1. You are going to use colors as you did before. As you enter into this kind of relaxation, tell your subconscious mind that each number counted will cause you to go at least a seventh of the way into relaxation such as you have just imagined. Remember the sequence:

The number 7—red
The number 6—orange
The number 5—yellow
The number 4—green
The number 3—blue
The number 2—purple
The number 1—violet

Now you know how easy it is. You have done it yourself, with your own thoughts, each thought acting as a cause for the effect of relaxation. Already you have been using your subconscious mind to work for you. Be sure that you notice this fact. You have been introducing relaxation thoughts to your subconscious mind, which has been creating a reality from them.

Now move on to a deeper level of relaxation, beyond what you learned in Chapter 4. You can establish deeper levels of consciousness by entering into the scene of nature where nothing can disturb you, nothing can bother you, with the exception that if there should be any emergency that requires your attention, you will easily be able to leave your relaxed state and take care of it.

Imagine yourself in your scene of nature, see yourself strolling along in this wonderful, wonderful place, unoccupied by any other person.... It's your secret place, a secret forest, a secret valley..... Wherever it may be, just imagine yourself there and feel the warmth of the air around you, and the warmth of the sunshine. . . . . Use all of your five senses to enjoy this place. Look around you and see everything there is to see. If there is any plant life, look at it. See the shrubs, the flowers, and the trees. . . . Notice the colors of other things around you such as the earth, and the ground cover, the rocks, the sand, whatever there is . . . Notice the sky and see how beautiful it looks . . . . . Perhaps there is water nearby in the form of a lake, a river, or a beach. Take it all in and listen to it, hear its sounds, the beautiful sounds of water, the sounds of nature . . . . The sounds of birds and animals, of the wind and the breeze. Hear all the sounds around you and become completely one with this environment . . . . . . Use your sense of smell and enjoy the aromas of this beautiful, sweet scene. Smell the plants, smell the earth and the water, the very air itself. Feel the wonderful sense of exhilaration that it gives you, the peaceful feeling of belonging here . . . . . .

Locate a lovely spot where you can settle down, a place where you can lie on the ground. Spread out a blanket and lie there looking up at the sky, totally at peace . . . . . . You see this beautiful, beautiful blue sky, powder-puff clouds just drifting along, and you feel at one with everything . . . And as you lie there on the blanket you have such a wonderful feeling about life, and about yourself. Thoughts go through your mind now that reflect your dreams and your wishes. You have dreams for yourself in the world of sports, you have hopes and aspirations. Let your eyes close and daydream for a while. Picture yourself living out, experiencing the wildest of your dreams. Just imagine yourself having fulfilled those dreams, those wishes . . . . See yourself performing now in the manner that you desire. The manner that, in truth, is within you to do, as you release your potential and the power of your mind . . . . . And you can release that power and potential through the subconscious mind by picturing yourself doing that which you dream of . . . . . .

See yourself performing and achieving the goals you prepared for this exercise. Imagine those goals realized, imagine every move, every motion, every technique perfectly executed. Imagine the feelings of confidence and exhilaration that go with performing to the optimum . . . . . Imagine the satisfaction of achievement, the response of your friends and family to your achievement . . . . . See yourself on top, having accomplished your goals in every respect . . . . . . Imagine this scene now in vivid detail, leaving out nothing. See yourself feeling the confidence that comes from knowing that you always knew you could do it! Imagine your fantastic performance seeming perfectly natural to you . . . . . .

In the days to follow, repeat this exercise. Learn to think of yourself as the person you have just been imagining . . . . . . Think of yourself as the person who always could, and always will, achieve your fondest dreams . . . . .

Develop a self-image consistent with, and in harmony with, your athletic and other goals. You will then see yourself as the person you wish to be, you will see yourself performing as you wish to perform, you will see yourself as the person who thinks, acts, and feels, consistent with the goals that you wish to realize. You will become the person you have been visualizing . . . . . .

In the days to follow you will continue to practice with your relaxation exercises . . . . . You will be able to achieve a deep and beautiful level of relaxation quickly and easily . . . . . You will do it more and more on your own . . . . . and you will soon be programming—most effectively—all of your goals into your subconscious mind . . . . . Soon you will be able to reenergize your body, to revitalize it and give it new strength and spirit . . . . . These relaxation exercises will enable you to accelerate healing should injuries occur, and to accelerate recovery from diseases . . . .

And now it is time to return once again to full alertness. But before you do, remind yourself that you are becoming better than ever at relaxing . . . . . And remember that you are learning to program your mind effectively. Because of that you will become successful in achieving all of your athletic goals. You are using—and will continue to use—all of the methods that you have been taught and that you have learned. You will use these methods successfully. You will achieve your goals, and it will be much easier than you ever dreamed . . . .

And now return yourself to full alertness by telling yourself that as you count back up from 1 to 7, each number will bring you at least one seventh of the way toward a very full and bright alertness. Each number will bring you part of the way back, a seventh of the way back to full alertness and vitality. You will return to a level of consciousness that will be exactly the right level for whatever activities are scheduled to come next.

When you have arrived all the way back to the number 7, take three deep breaths, and on the peak of intake of that third breath, open your eyes, smile, stretch, feel alive and alert, refreshed, revitalized, reenergized, and rested. It will be as if you have had a wonderful nap, and you will feel confident that your efforts are working!

☆   ☆   ☆   ☆   ☆

Mental Project for Chapter 5

To assist you in realizing the power of the subconscious mind and its invisible ability to bring your goals to pass, try this experiment for a week. Each night as you retire, establish your usual routine of ensuring you will be awakened at the necessary time (i.e., setting your clock or having someone call you). But, in addition, this week mentally program a different waking time. Tell your subconscious that you wish to awaken with its help fifteen minutes earlier than your clock awakens you or someone calls. Look at your clock and "see" the time that you wish your subconscious to awaken you.

Try this each night for a week. When you are successful two or three mornings in a row, set a new time, one in which you normally would not awaken, such as 3:30 A.M. Tell yourself this is a test and that you wish to be awakened at that time, just long enough to know that there is an active intelligence within you that will respond to your wishes. Then you will return to perfect rest and sleep until your usual wake-up time in the morning. Be sure you also "look" at the time you wish to awaken before going to sleep.

Not only will this exercise help to convince you of the reality of a subconscious power, but it is a good first step in training yourself to use that power.

6 How to Program Your Goals

> Great living starts with a picture, held in your imagination, of what you would like to do or be.
>
> HENRY EMERSON FOSDICK[1]

Over the years you may have noticed some athletes withdrawing just prior to a competitive event. You may have seen them sitting with eyes closed and to all appearances resting, quieting themselves, or even praying. It is more likely, however, they were "psyching in" for their event. They may have used a scientific, systematic approach, or it might have been something they picked up from friends and had decided to give it a try. Either way, it probably helped, a little bit or a lot, depending on how well the Mental Dynamics were understood and applied.

By reading the previous chapter, you have been preparing yourself in greater depth to use mental programming techniques, not only for pre-event preparation but for long-range benefits and goals too. You will now learn how to prepare yourself, not just for current events, but for the next year and the years to follow, for those major long-range goals that you dream of fulfilling.

USE YOUR MENTAL TAPE RECORDER

Pre-event "psyching in" or preparation can do for the mind the same thing that stretching and warming up can do for the body. The real mental training and conditioning should already be complete through previous months of effort. *Last-minute "psyching up" has as much value mentally as last-minute training and conditioning has physically.*

To be highly effective in mentally programming your goals, think of your mind as similar to a tape recorder. A recorder is equipped with means

[1] Maxwell Maltz, *Psycho-Cybernetics* (Englewood Cliffs, N.J.: Prentice-Hall, Inc., 1960).

for input, such as a microphone, and output, such as speakers. Underline, in your mind, the principle that nothing will issue forth from the machine that has not been previously introduced. Output is a reflection of input. Put another way, tape recorders, computers, and the human mind all work on the GIGO rule: garbage in = garbage out!

Thus, we observe that the mind's output can be influenced by input, which you can control, once you learn how. Think of all behavior, including physical, athletic activity, as output, or a playback of the human computer. Thought is input and processed through the mind until behavior or performance results. Mental output, including performance, is almost unlimited in its diversity.

The kind of self-image data about you as an athlete that has been introduced and stored on your mental tapes, consciously or unconsciously, *strongly influences how you play or perform athletically.* Other stored data concerning yourself, your sport, your competition, plus a host of other related factors, determines ultimately what your body will do and how well it will do it. If stored data says you are at a disadvantage competing on the road, then you are likely to be so. On the other hand, Mental Dynamics will teach you to change that data in the storage bank so that it says, "You enjoy playing away and you always automatically perform even better when away from home." And, as a result, you will greatly improve the likelihood of realizing that goal. You can even overcome the effects of jet lag by using input data that says, "You get more energy and enthusiasm when traveling."

These are a few of many overlooked factors not directly connected with athletics that significantly affect athletic performance. Your performance, even your life itself, will reflect the data previously introduced to your subconscious computer mind. Remember, *you can do anything if the data in your computer supports your goal. You can be anything at all if your mental computer is programmed to be that kind of person. There are no true limitations placed on you other than those of natural law.* Any other limitations are those of your own thinking. You can develop. You can achieve. You can excel. You can be more decisive, consistent. Anything at all is possible when the appropriate data is in the subconscious computer.

You have chosen your goals and are committed to them. Now, as you provide your mental computer the correct supporting data, you can eventually achieve those goals. You can become a completely successful athlete.

As you select goals, which will be your future output, one of the prime concerns will be your input. Be certain that all your input thoughts relate favorably to those defined goals. Assure that they are in harmony with and supporting of your goals of maximum athletic development and performance.

Remember, thought is the first cause of all effects. *Thought* is the basic tool in mental programming. You will present your goal-thoughts to the subconscious computerlike mind to enable the desired output to emerge. Your subconscious will convert your goal-thoughts into a reality.

Thought, that untouchable, intangible essence, is more real than anything we can imagine, yet because it seems unreal to our physical senses, its power and impact are overlooked by most. You, however, can be different. You will appreciate and use that seemingly unbelievable power that everyone has: that power of thought, properly controlled and channeled. You will be among the elite few who exploit that power to better yourself athletically and personally, and in many other ways as well.

METHOD FOR PROGRAMMING GOALS

The most basic systematic method of mentally programming long- and short-range goals is found in the following simple steps: (1) schedule two sessions a day for mental programming; (2) create proper conditions enabling easy introduction of thoughts to your subconscious; (3) use affirmations; (4) use creative imagery; (5) use emotionalization. Now let's take a look at these steps in more detail.

STEP 1: SCHEDULE MENTAL PROGRAMMING TIME TWICE A DAY. This is an important step for the purpose of ensuring that mental programming gets done and becomes a habit. Make your programming a high-priority *must*, one that precedes all other requirements of the day. We suggest mental conditioning take place early in the morning and toward the end of the day.

Before reading on, please fill out a time schedule card similar to the one shown in the Appendix. That will give you a clear idea of when you will be doing your programming. Post your card where you can see it and it will remind you to do your "mentals." Soon they will become a habit.

STEP 2: CREATE A PROPER MENTAL ENVIRONMENT. This means creating one or more of the situations that allow for the easy introduction of thought to your subconscious mind as outlined in Chapter 3, which described the various kinds of hypnotic states. These usable states, or conditions, include the trances (which we will not use), repetition, emotion, relaxation (our preferred method), and sleep. There are several conditions that can be easily used for mental programming. One is the morning trance state, which we all experience. You may also use repetition. We will discuss that later on. Another of the conditions you may use is mental relaxation. We strongly favor this approach because of the additional benefits that can be derived from relaxation besides mental programming. You have read about relaxation training in Chapter 4. If you have followed instructions carefully and practiced regularly, you are ready to use mental relaxation as a basic condition for mental programming.

Now you are ready for STEP 3: USE AFFIRMATION. An affirmation is a carefully worded statement you will use to present your goals to the subconscious mind. Your goals will relate to your development as an athlete and as a person. Repeat aloud this definition of affirmation, and make sure you thoroughly understand it, for it is essential to your success with it.

An affirmation is a carefully worded statement of a goal, presented to your subconscious as if it, the goal, had already been achieved. In most cases you will present it to your subconscious mind in the present, rather than the future, tense. Although intellectually you know your goal is in the future, successful mental programming requires that it be stated as a present tense, already realized fact. This is because the subconscious mind by nature is literal, just as a computer is literal. It receives your data exactly as you present it. If you affirm vaguely in the future tense as follows: "I will be more adaptable," the literal subconscious will find that too vague to work with in the present. The affirmation must be, "I adjust and adapt quickly to all situations." You should not say things like, "I will give one-hundred-percent effort," or "I am going to try to accept constructive criticism." Rather, your affirmations should be, "I always give one-hundred-percent effort," and "I gladly accept, and use, constructive criticism."

The only future tense affirmations the subconscious will work with are those in which specific dates are used. For instance, "I will master the basic rules handbook by July twelfth," or "I will begin my weight training program on November tenth," or "I will be ready in all respects for the big contest on July fourth." You will remember that our fictitious athlete, Joe, used time-pegged future tense affirmations in Chapter 5.

You will use *repetition* as an effective condition for affirming your goals. As you affirm your goal-thoughts repeatedly to your subconscious mind, it will receive them and move to create a realization for them. Repetition and affirmations will join as partners to lead you to activity, performance, and perfection that are harmonious with your goals.

Any idea, plan, or purpose may be placed in the subconscious mind through the repetition of thought. Emile Coué, father of autosuggestion, said, "Every idea which enters the mind, *when accepted*, is transformed by it [the mind] into a reality and forms henceforth a permanent element in our life." Coué, incidentally, was the same man who had half of America, in the twenties, looking at themselves in the mirror and repeating his suggestion that "every day, in every way, I am getting better and better!"

Thus, the repetition of a positive affirmation, idea, thought, or suggestion has the power to suppress, inhibit, cancel, or correct old negative thoughts or ideas. Self-image, self-esteem, health, physical abilities, emotional relationships with others, including coaches and players, even the competition, can all be affected by the repetition of a positive affirmation. Negations or the negative thoughts carried in our mental computers with respect to these same areas have the same power and are in fact the source of limitation, failure, inhibition, fear, disappointment, and frustration for all of us.

A positive affirmation creates an attitude or a posture in life that says, "I can." Thus, an affirmation that says, "I am a superb golfer and do a superb job of putting," has the power, when received by the subconscious mind, of correcting any self-image data that says, "I always goof my putts," or "I never win." A positive affirmation with respect to your tennis serve, your football passing, your baseball hitting, or whatever it may be has the power to correct any old data that may spell out limitation.

When you have envisioned a goal and created its attainment on the plane of the mind, nothing can keep you from realizing that goal other than the creation of failure or limitation on the plane of the mind.

Mental programming is a gradual process. The results are also gradual, but real. Mental programming does not necessarily result in immediate or dramatic change, especially if it involves correcting old ideas and habit patterns of thought about yourself, your sport, or ideas about what is, or is not, possible. In many ways it is similar to posthypnotic suggestion; it is not as fast or dramatic, but it is more permanent.

Affirmations are repeated out loud, especially for newcomers to their use. Repetition is one of the factors that also help move the thoughts into the subconscious.

You will find included in the Appendix a list of suggested affirmations to help you program your goals. The numbers on this list correspond with the numbers on the Mental Dynamics Suggested Goals List, discussed in Chapter 5 and also shown in the Appendix. Remember, however, that you can—and often should—construct your own affirmations.

The following items are important to keep in mind when creating your own affirmations. They are a valuable checklist that you should use because it is vital that you be technically correct. If carelessly done, your affirmations may be ineffective or even cause contrary results. Therefore, pay heed to the following:

A. The subconscious is literal, therefore:
    1. Keep in the present tense (except when target dates are included).
    2. When possible, state affirmations positively. Avoid negatives.
    3. If an affirmation is worded negatively, *do not use imagery with it.*
B. Wherever possible, construct affirmations as a self-image statement beginning with:
        I or I am . . .
        I always enjoy . . .
C. Make them permanent: I always . . .
D. Include words that suggest emotion: I always enjoy . . .
E. Keep sentences simple and brief. Several short sentences are better than one long one.

STEP 4: USE CREATIVE IMAGERY. Creative imagery is also a means of presenting your goal-thoughts to your subconscious mind. It is probably most effective as a supplement to using affirmations. You can imagine your goals in much the same way you affirm them, but with more detail and feeling. When practicing creative imagery, it is important that you carefully define and describe the goal, in advance, so that you will know how the goal should be when realized. This allows for easier and more effective imagery. Imagine how you will feel and experience your goal, when achieved, as this is an important part of the data that should be programmed in your mental computer. It is important to prethink what it will be like when each goal is achieved so that you can imagine the emotional satisfaction that will result. Imagine, for example, the supreme, relaxed confidence of having achieved consistency or from having intensified and strengthened your concentration. Imagine being able to go through training and conditioning drills with a sense of achievement, satisfaction, and even enjoyment. Imagine making quick decisions. Imagine perfecting the moves that are unique to your sport. Imagine goals such as these in detail until you feel the feelings you will have when they are actually realized. You can perfect these goals and others when the right data is in your mental computer.

Creative imagery employs the law of subconscious teleology. This law says, "When the end or the goal has been defined and can be seen, the subconscious will find the means for its realization."[2] Thus, a thought or an idea such as an affirmation has an even greater impact on the subconscious mind when it is accompanied by imagery that is consistent and reinforcing of the affirmation.

To the subconscious mind the act of imagery is the same as the act itself, for the subconscious does not distinguish between real and imagined. This is very important. We can practice anything in the imagination and improve our performance significantly by that approach alone. Thus, in addition to visualizing long-range goals, you can also practice in the imagination your various techniques. You can practice confidence, positive attitudes, and a host of other behaviors that normally require actual practice and experience. You can practice each and every goal in your mind—exactly as you wish it.

Many tests of this principle have been made. One was a study of the effects of mental practice on sinking basketball free throws. One group of students actually practiced shooting free throws every day for twenty days and were scored on the first and last day. A second group was scored on the first and last day and engaged in no practice of any kind. A third group was rated on the first day and then spent twenty minutes a day imagining that

[2]Charles Baudouin, *Suggestion and Auto-suggestion* (New York: Dodd, Mead & Company; London: Allen & Unwin Publishers Ltd., 1922).

they were throwing the ball into the basket. In their mind, if they missed, they would imagine that they had corrected their aim accordingly. This group was then tested again twenty days later.

The first group, which actually practiced with the ball twenty minutes every day, improved their scoring by 24 percent. The second group, which had no sort of practice, showed no improvement whatever. The third group, which practiced free-throw shooting in their imagination only, improved their scoring by 23 percent.

STEP 5: USE EMOTION. An important factor in the programming of goals in the subconscious mind is emotion. We have already discussed the value of strong goal feelings in the last chapter. Those same techniques can now be used to help program your goals. Up to now you have considered mental relaxation and imagery as the important steps in the programming process. These steps can serve to activate the subconscious mind into causing a realization of your goals. However, the clincher, in mental programming, is considered by many to be emotion.

Emotion can serve as the catalyst, the igniter for getting the wheels of previous programming in motion. Emotion lights the fire of enthusiasm. It keeps the goal in consciousness. It triggers goal-directed activity. Emotion is the essence of motivation.

Literally and truly, emotion is and has always been the power force that impels us toward our greatest achievements. This same power of emotion is at work on the negative side. Negative emotion is the power that has led many to their greatest folly, if not downfall. Emotion can be mastered and harnessed. Thus, negative emotion can, and should, be controlled if it leads to behaviors that are counter to your goals. Positive emotion can be generated and used. Desire and wanting are positive emotions which, when attached to a goal, give the force behind achievement that goes beyond intellectually knowing about the goal. The subconscious, through which your goals will be realized, is activated and energized by emotional feelings.

Often, as you visualize your goal in some detail, you will find that *feeling* will also follow automatically. Frederick Pierce, in his book *Mobilizing the Mid-Brain*, refers to the law of the dominant effect:

> An idea always tends toward a realization at any given time. There is available in the brain, only a certain amount of energy which is always attracted to the strongest emotional wish feeling present. Thus, when a person is experiencing the emotion of pleasure, and danger intrudes, danger is stronger and subdues the pleasure instinct, which disappears instantly if the danger is great. Thus, to achieve the greatest results from a suggestion it must be attached to an emotion of the instinct group. Having such energy capacity is to surmount any other then likely to be active in the mind. The desire for success is an excellent

motivation for use in connection with suggestion. Emotion can best be aroused by visualization. A description or story emphasizing the content of the emotion rather than the feeling.[3]

Move in the direction of mustering feeling and *excitement* for each goal that you have chosen. Want it, desire it with enthusiasm, with a passion, if you dare, and let nothing or no one deny you that goal.

REVIEW OF THE GOAL-SETTING METHOD

Now that you have examined the five steps of the mental programming process, let's briefly review the basics of Mental Dynamics as taught in these last two chapters.

Start with the idea of goal setting, which includes the seven steps outlined in Chapter 5. These are the self-survey, selecting specific goals, defining those goals, defining a plan of action, making a firm commitment, developing enthusiasm for the goals, and finally presenting the goals to the subconscious (mental programming). This final step of mental programming is subdivided into the five steps discussed in this chapter. In summary, they are:

1. Scheduling mental programming time in which you set aside at least two periods each day for practicing mental programming techniques.
2. Creating a proper mental climate for mental programming. This means creating or using existing situations and conditions that allow for easy introduction of your goal-thoughts to the subconscious. There are natural periods during the day that are ideal for effective mental programming. We suggest using time as soon after awakening in the morning as possible. This allows you to take advantage of the hypnoidal state that exists when first awakened. The second best time for mental programming is immediately before retiring in the evening. A third natural time is shortly after lunch. In each event, select a quiet place away from sounds and disturbances. You may also create a mentally relaxed state by either using your own relaxation tapes or inducing relaxation on your own. Either way, the idea is to create a state of mental stillness when your intellectual mind is not questioning the affirmations used. Place yourself, seated, in an upright position, with your eyes closed, unless you need to check your notes. If you are already drowsy or sleepy, sit with your back straight to counteract any tendency to drift into sleep.
3. After achieving mental stillness, repeat your affirmations aloud. They should be spoken loud enough for your ears to hear. Each affirmation is repeated ten times during each sitting for three weeks. Thereafter, you may reduce the repetitions to five.

[3]New York: E. P. Dutton & Co., Inc., 1924. Copyright renewal, 1952, by Frederick Pierce. Reprinted by permission of the publisher, E. P. Dutton, Inc.,

4. Creative imagery. After each affirmation has been repeated, pause and then imagine the goal that you affirmed, using as much detail as possible. Mentally employ as many of the senses as you can. Live the experience in your mind as fully as you can so that you can actually experience the appropriate feelings. If you imagine running a cross-country race, you may even feel your heart beating faster and your legs beginning to ache. Summon as much feeling as possible. This is done by living the scene in your mind as totally as you can.

If you have previously prepared for your imagery—that is, if you know exactly what the scene and detail will be—the actual doing it need not take more than a minute or two. When it is completed, proceed to the next goal by first affirming the goal and then visualizing it. Then on to the next goal, and so forth. When you have finished programming all your goals, simply return to full alertness in the manner you learned in Chapter 4, about relaxation.

5. The clincher in mental programming is emotion, for it creates enthusiasm and sustains motivation; and these are important building blocks of *desire.* One must honestly desire to achieve his goal, and emotion helps to generate desire—especially for those goals that are not by nature very exciting.

In the next section of this chapter (the relaxation exercise) we have included an actual run-through of the steps just outlined, expanding on the relaxation methods discussed in Chapters 4 and 5. Do not be concerned with any apparent variations in technique, because variety is possible when you are familiar with the fundamentals. Use the relaxation exercises often and they will benefit you greatly.

Before proceeding to subsequent chapters, be certain that you have practiced your programming technique twice a day—every day!

Relaxation Exercise for Chapter 6

In the Chapter 5 relaxation exercise you mastered the general techniques of relaxation. Now you are ready to learn how to mentally program your athletic goals through the use of two new techniques—affirmation and visualization.

Before proceeding with this training exercise, we would like to instruct you on the procedures to follow. In this particular exercise, you will do the lion's share of the relaxing on your own. This time we will only cue you along the way. The goal of this whole series of relaxation exercises is to teach you how to bring yourself to whatever level of relaxation you wish. This time you will accomplish relaxation almost entirely on your own. In addition, before proceeding, you should prepare yourself as follows:

1. Have a place or scene of nature that you retreat to.
2. Fix in your mind someplace where you plan to be doing your mental programming each morning and evening.
3. Identify five specific goals to work with.
4. Have five affirmations, one for each goal.
5. Have five supporting visualizations for those affirmations, ready to use with this exercise.

Now prepare to enter into a level of relaxation that is ideal for mental programming purposes. Begin this relaxation exercise by placing yourself in the proper position. Then in order to eliminate any surface tension that may exist, proceed with the breathing exercise that you have learned.

☆   ☆   ☆   ☆   ☆

Breathe in to a count of four, 1 . . . 2 . . . 3 . . . 4 . . . , hold for a count of two, 1 . . . 2 . . . , then sigh the breath out . . . . . Visualize all tensions, cares, and concerns going out with the breath as you exhale. Feel the pleasure of the exhalation . . . Remember to allow the rate of speed of your count to approximate the rate of speed of your pulse.

Having accomplished that, use your imagination to bring relaxation to both mind and body by remembering how relaxed you can be. Remember the hands, and the fingers, and the toes, and the legs . . . . Remember the shoulders, the chest, and the upper and lower abdomen . . . . Just remember how relaxed you can be in those areas. Remember the back muscles, upper and lower . . . . All up and down the spinal column . . . . The muscles at the base of the skull and at the back of the neck . . . . Remember how still and quiet your mind has been . . . and imagine yourself in that state of relaxation right now . . . Imagine your entire body completely, totally relaxed, just as you remembered it . . . Feel the pleasure of your relaxation . . . Feel yourself slipping, sliding, and sinking into that serene, tranquil relaxation . . . . .

Now you are ready to move on to the next part, which is counting down, in your mind, from 7 to 1. Tell yourself that each number you count brings you even closer to perfect relaxation. Each number will bring you another seventh of the way toward the perfect level of relaxation that you have chosen for the exercise. Begin with a sighing breath and count down from 7 to 1 as you've been taught. Each number will guide you toward perfect relaxation . . . .

You find that you are able to move more rapidly now because you have practiced regularly with relaxation. It doesn't take long to relax anymore. It happens easily and quickly.

As you come to the end of your count, let your mind easily move into your scene of nature. Project yourself completely to your scene of nature. Use all your senses. See, hear, feel, smell, and experience all of the scenery around you .... Experience this wonderful scene in every way you can. Be there, feel it—be one with this scene .... Take your time—be thorough and complete .... Finally, place yourself on a blanket on this ideal spot where you can lie down and look at the sky. Daydream and let your mind wander .... As your mind drifts in this wonderful, serene, tranquil setting, let it wander to your place at home or work, or wherever it may be that you are planning to do your mental programming. Let your mind wander to that scene so that you can totally imagine yourself there .... It may be a bedroom. It may be an office. Wherever it happens to be, look around and see the room .... Use all your senses to actually put you in that room as far as your mind is concerned ..... As you are now in that room, imagine yourself sitting comfortably in your chair with your eyes closed. You are mentally relaxing yourself. Imagine yourself going through the procedures that you have just gone through to become relaxed. Imagine yourself breathing in to a count of four .... Holding for a count of two .... And sighing it out .... Feel the pleasure of those relaxation exhalations .... Imagine yourself remembering relaxation .... Remember it happening .... Flowing over you .... Imagine yourself counting down from 7 to 1 .... Becoming even more relaxed as you do so. Imagine yourself in that chair now, projecting yourself to a scene of nature .... Imagine yourself now, completely relaxed and ready to do your affirmations and visualizations ....

Take the first of your five goals and affirm it. Affirm it to yourself in that room. Imagine yourself in the room, repeating aloud—but softly—your first affirmation, whatever it may be, ten times ..... Imagine yourself visualizing that goal as completely achieved and realized. Imagine yourself in successful action, realizing, succeeding, achieving with that specific goal ...

Now in your mind imagine yourself repeating your second affirmation. In your mind hear yourself repeating aloud—but softly—the second affirmation and proceed to visualize it, to bring it into imagery .....

Then continue on with the third, fourth, and fifth goals in the same fashion. Take the necessary time to do so .....

As the subconscious receives your goal-thoughts in the form of affirmation and imagery, it will—in a steady, subtle, gradual way—work toward bringing those goal-thoughts into reality .... Remember also that as you visualize yourself achieving those goals, the subconscious cannot discern between real and imagined. So it records your perfected visualization as a successful experience. Thus, it will be ready to give you positive feedback in your next actual athletic effort. As you sit in the room completing your mental programming, get the feeling of confidence that your programming is working. Feel that your efforts with these techniques are—and will continue—working! Allow time, reinforced by repetition each morning and each evening. Know that your mental programming works and remember that you may do your mental programming in the special manner described here. Or you can go to your room and simply follow the steps that you have just visualized.

Now in your awareness, allow yourself to return to your scene of nature. Leave the mental room you were in and return to your scene of nature. In this scene see the sights around you once again, everything, including the sky and trees .... From your scene of nature, return yourself to the place where you started this exercise. Then very easily and slowly, on your own and in the manner you have been taught, return yourself back all the way to full alertness. Count back up from 1 to 7 ...... Then on the completion of the seven-count, take three deep breaths, and on the peak of intake of the third breath, open your eyes, smile and stretch and feel in tune with life.

☆   ☆   ☆   ☆   ☆

How to Know When Your Mental Programming Is Working

Many new students of mental programming wish to know how they can tell when the system is working. How can they be sure the goal wouldn't have been realized without the programming activity?

The easiest way to know that your subconscious is working with your goals is "to notice." *Notice* that things "just happen." *Notice* that you act or react, in certain situations, differently from the way you used to, and notice after the fact. You will notice that the goal you programmed just seemed to happen. That you did not need to make it happen with force or power.

In other words, behavior or performance that you formerly forcibly had to make happen now seems to "just happen." Certainly you helped. You did something. But the results seem to be more natural and subtle. There is nothing dramatic, but it does happen and it is real. As one young athlete said, "After that eighteen-hour flight, I couldn't believe it. I affirmed it and it just happened. No jet lag. I didn't even realize it was working until after the race. There was absolutely no sign of fatigue. It works!"

You will know that your mental programming is effective because you will notice changes, after they happen. You'll notice feelings changing for the better. You'll notice little things at first, and they will accumulate and grow!

It may seem like coincidence, but most likely it is not. It will be the result of steady, consistent programming, working in you just like post-hypnotic suggestion.

You will notice your averages improving, confidence growing, techniques refining. It will seem as if they just happen without any great effort. Change, growth, and development will occur. You will notice as it happens or afterward. Be pleased about it. Enjoy the results and be sure to thank your subconscious for what it did.

The changes that occur as a result of these methods are usually gradual and subtle, and as such, it can be more difficult to see them at times. Generally, changes in self-image traits may take one to three weeks. Each person is unique and will have to determine for himself how long it takes. With repeated continuous practice, the effects of mental programming are swifter and more dramatic.

Mental Project for Chapter 6

This project will give you an opportunity to see how your subconscious mind and Mental Dynamics can be a lot of fun and will give you an advantage in a gamelike situation. You might even be able to make a few dollars if you're a betting person.

Take an ordinary deck of playing cards and a wastebasket, or similar container. Place the basket about six feet from a chair and then sit down with the playing cards in hand. One by one, try to toss the cards into the container. When you have tossed them all, write down the number of cards that ended up in the basket. Then sit down in the chair, close your eyes, and relax. Mentally picture yourself increasing your score by five cards. You need only picture this result for about fifteen seconds, then you will be ready to try again.

Once again, take the deck of cards in hand and sit down on the chair. Relax your mind and body before the flip of each card. Some people find that closing the eyes during this moment of relaxation is even better.

In almost all cases your second score will be close to the one you visualized during your fifteen-second programming session. Have fun!

7 The Secret

Your self-regard, and the value you attach to that regard, will
affect your performance more than any other thing.

JAMES BENNETT[1]

The greatest secret of success is yet to be told. Up to this point you have
learned important concepts and techniques that have been known and used
by great athletes throughout the ages. Some of them, in the past, have been
concealed and treated as secret. We, too, have referred to some earlier materials as the secret behind certain accomplishments.

Yet one may ask, "How can these precepts be considered secret when
we are so public about them?" This is a fair question. The answer, to follow,
is both obvious and mysterious.

To understand fully the secret and gain the special benefits of these
hidden ideas and methods, one must continue to study, practice, and meditate upon the material contained in this book. Do not skim through once or
twice, but consider them over and over many times, in as much depth as
possible. Each new reading will reveal new thoughts, new meanings not
apparent previously. Some concepts may take months, even years, to "come
alive" in consciousness.

KNOWING ABOUT VERSUS KNOWING

The answer is partly found in the scriptural passage "They have eyes, but see
not, and ears, but hear not." The meaning of this can be found in earlier
chapters where you were urged to carefully study as you read, if you wished
to take full advantage of Mental Dynamics. In fact, to study so well that you
would not only know *about* relaxation, revitalization, goal setting, mental

[1]From an address given at the Washington State Athletic Director's Association
convention, Seattle, Washington, 1978.

68

programming, and all the other concepts, but you would learn to *know* them. There is a tremendous, though subtle, difference between *knowing about* something and really *knowing* that something.

Knowing is to move knowledge past the intellect, to go beyond intellectualizing and move knowledge into the subconscious mind. Knowing about something is simply the possession of knowledge. Knowing something is to become one with it; to make it so much a part of your life and consciousness that you become a part of it, influenced and guided by the knowledge itself. It is such that your reactions, related to the "something" you *know*, become almost instinctive, occurring without conscious thought. To take it a step further, it is like the driver-education teacher who told his students, "When you finish this course, you will know a lot about driving, but only when your reactions to emergencies become instinctive will you actually know how to drive."

Therefore, we say again that *knowing about* something = possession of knowledge. But *knowing* = being possessed by that knowledge. Do you understand this? It is not easy, but it is important. If you have trouble grasping that meaning, read this portion of the chapter many times, write it down, and meditate upon it until it sinks in. *For therein is found the secret!*

Thousands upon thousands of people have heard and read of the secrets contained in this book. Only a few have learned them and have come to know and live them. The choice is yours: know about or *know*!

THE SECRET OF HARMONY

You are now ready for the other great secret, for there are two. This is a truth we regard as the most important of all. It is the secret called *harmony*. To discuss harmony in full would require more pages than this book permits. If you desire a more in-depth study of it, inquire of the Mental Dynamics Basic Life Enrichment Tape series.[2] Here we will discuss harmony with you in abbreviated form, but with all the essentials included. Be prepared for many readings and much study to grasp its deep and fantastic implications.

The secret is this: *All living things seek to be in harmony with their own nature. To the degree harmony is achieved, optimal functioning and performance is possible. To the degree harmony is blocked, optimal functioning is impaired.*

All living things have their nature. To the extent that they live in harmony with their nature, they thrive, grow, and expand. A cactus growing in the desert has its special nature by living in arid soil, and is in harmony with

[2] Human Factors Seminars, Inc., P.O. Box 10185, Bainbridge Island, WA, 98110.

it. And so it thrives. Transplanted into the damp rain forests of the Pacific Northwest, the cactus would quickly experience great disharmony. It would soon die. Likewise, a cedar transplanted from the rain forests to the hot, dry desert country would also suffer severe disharmony, malfunction, and death.

We human beings also have a nature. We have a physical and a psychological nature. To be in harmony at the physical level requires proper nutrition, exercise, rest, conditioning, and the right amounts of oxygen and water. At the psychological level, we possess what is called human nature. Human nature has qualities common to all. When these qualities are driven out of harmony to some degree, dysfunction will result to that same degree— socially, emotionally, and physically. When in harmony, these same qualities allow optimal performance. *To the extent an athlete is in harmony with his physical and psychological nature, he is able to maximize his athletic performance.*

Though many people may achieve a large degree of physical harmony through appropriate nutrition, rest, and exercise, it is insufficient if the psychological nature is not also in harmony. Most people are not really acquainted with their psychological harmony. *Every aspect of human performance is affected by how much we are in or out of harmony with our psychological nature.* Athletic activity is no exception. In fact, for many athletes, the outcome of competitive performance is affected by this factor more than any other, because it is the least understood.

THE POWER OF SELF-ESTEEM

The first and most important part of our human nature with which we must be in harmony is *self-esteem*. Self-esteem may be defined as "how you feel about yourself." Some will say that self-esteem is how you like yourself. We agree with both of these definitions. Self-esteem is how you like yourself, and how you like yourself affects how you feel about yourself.

Self-esteem is also how you feel about life or how you love live itself. It is how you enjoy living. This definition refers not only to the enjoyment of living but to the *how* of living as well. How you enjoy life and living is how you enjoy being yourself. When you enjoy being yourself, or when you like yourself, you enjoy life. Because, as it turns out, you are life. Have you ever thought of it in quite that fashion? "I am life!"

When you value or love life, you enjoy and value yourself as well. When you value and enjoy yourself, you are a happy person—more secure, comfortable, and at peace with yourself and the world. You have a healthy self-esteem, which is the most important factor in the psychological, emotional, and social health of any individual. Self-esteem is as essential to the attainment and maintenance of superb self-confidence and psychological health as proper rest, food, and exercise are to the attainment of a healthy and competitive body.

Historically, not enough attention has been given to self-esteem, perhaps because it is an invisible and intangible thing. Self-esteem cannot be grasped or experienced through the senses as are other things. You cannot physically handle self-esteem, nor taste or eat it.

In fact, many people discourage self-esteem out of fear that it will lead to self-dwelling or conceit. On the contrary, truly healthy and appropriate self-esteem eliminates behavior usually adjudged as conceited. A healthy self-esteem is a prerequisite for sustained, successful performance in virtually every category of life, including personal and athletic achievement.

Self-esteem is an allowing force, not just a state of being or experience. And it is also reinforced and propagated by the very success that it breeds. A strong, healthy self-esteem is part of emotional health. Those who lack it tend to be nervous, fearful, anxiety-ridden, depressed, discouraged, or prone to illness and failure in their personal lives, in their business, or in their athletic career. We are reminded of the man who said, "The world is a tuxedo, and I'm the shorts!"

On the other hand, those who have healthy self-esteem are usually happy, comfortable, relaxed individuals with a greater sense of inner peace and calm. They are more comfortable in their relationships with others, a factor affecting morale among teammates and relationships between coaches and players. These people tend to be more successful in achieving athletic goals as well as goals in other areas of their lives. *They do well because they like themselves, and do not depend on doing well to like themselves.* They can accept setbacks, disappointments, and rejections more easily. Their dependence on others is reduced as they develop greater mental freedom and strength.

Individuals with strong, healthy self-esteem have greater satisfaction in their sports activity. These people can accept criticism and suggestion. They can take advice. They listen. They are not intimidated by the jeering of crowds. And they are largely immune to the psyching efforts of opposing players. They enjoy all aspects of their athletic experience and are more prone to success.

When you bring this healthy, happy, confident self to different areas of life—whether it be in your athletic pursuit, family, or job—you enjoy doing what you're doing and you do it well, because you are that kind of person. That kind of person is free to do a better job. The key here, the secret, is that when you enjoy being yourself, you enjoy doing whatever you're doing. You do it better, you learn it faster, and you develop faster. When you enjoy being yourself in all ways, you can be a better athlete. That kind of person is the one you bring to the different situations of your life. You do not require those situations to bring you all the enjoyment of life. You bring happy attitudes and feelings to all situations as opposed to those individuals whose self-esteem or happiness is dependent upon the situations, or the condition itself. The latter person depends on the job, achievement in sports, or other things in order to feel good about himself.

We are all familiar with the student who must cheat to achieve the grade necessary to make him feel good about himself. Unlike the pragmatic athlete who cheats simply to maintain eligibility, this student is usually far above average. But a B+ grade is not good enough, so he cheats to "become" an A student in order to feel good about himself.

There are also many examples of both amateur and professional athletes who suffer nervous breakdowns trying to achieve a level of play somewhere beyond them. Instead of being content with their skills—often very good—they strive for a level beyond their abilities. Because they are so dependent on that "crutch" to develop an acceptable self-image, they become frustrated, and in time their mental health is impaired.

All people long to know and experience their value—free from the uncertainty and dependence on situations, conditions, and other people. So long as one is dependent on others, or things, there will never be complete satisfaction. For there is always the painful, subtle uncertainty and realization that people, things, and conditions are but props, any one of which can be removed without notice.

If you practice this type of conditional self-esteem, depending excessively on props, you will be vulnerable to inhibition, tension, anxiety, and fear, all of which diminish your ability to perform at optimal capacity. To the degree you are dependent on things, situations, or people to like yourself, you are vulnerable; for these props, on which you depend, can easily be withdrawn. When that occurs, self-esteem, supported by those props, may soon come crashing down. If winning is a prop, if praise is a prop for self-esteem and is depended on to excess, then losing and criticism can spiral you into a depression.

Another reaction of these people is to become angry while participating in sports. Bad play drives them to anger because it destroys their self-image, which is such a vital prop to their self-esteem. They lose their poise and concentration and, most often, the event as well. In a similar fashion, you see those depending on approval, good looks, beautiful bodies, and sharp minds suffering a loss of self-esteem when those props are lost to them by virtue of accident or age. An athlete depending on crowd approval for self-esteem may be jeered instead of cheered, and thus may lose his confidence or be otherwise emotionally shaken by the experience. The athlete who brings the happy, confident self to the crowd, rather than having the crowd make him happy, can enjoy his sport far better—and would normally perform better.

One asks, "Why is this so universally essential?" What is it that has people struggling to know their worth and value? To us the answer is found in the simple premise that all human life is by its nature pure, unconditional worth and value. All life is naturally precious, unconditionally! Life is of worth and value just because it is life, just for the being, and for no other reason. It is part of the nature of life itself.

It is also our belief that all living things seek, with whatever means possible, to live in harmony with their nature, which is to say they seek to know and experience themselves as of worth and value. When this is achieved, they are indeed at peace, relaxed, and at ease. They achieve inner tranquillity and serenity. They are in harmony. They are free again to perform naturally, freely, and in optimal ways. When they are not in harmony with their nature, and are uncertain of their worth, they experience tension, anxiety, fear, sometimes pain, and often the frustration uniquely found in not measuring up to what they know or feel is their inner potential. They may experience inhibition.

We *need* to feel worth and value. We *need* to feel as if we are something good, something right. Living in harmony with our nature is a *need* that we all strive to meet in whatever way we can. Athletics is one of those ways.

The fundamental nature of the human beast is threefold. All life by its very nature is of great value. Living in harmony with our value has been termed having healthy *self-esteem*. The other two features of our nature are *creative potential* and *freedom*. These last two are not discussed in detail in this book, although creative potential is addressed in Chapter 13.

In summary, you can see by now that it is most important—for the good life and great success in all areas of life—that each person be in harmony with each of those segments of his nature.

The development of a healthy self-esteem is essential to your success in sports. And this book, through the mental programming techniques you have learned, will help you to do that. First, you choose the goal. In this case, the goal of self-esteem. Define this goal carefully, as you have learned, so that you can visualize yourself as a person of great worth—just because you are life itself. Then, following all the steps outlined in previous chapters, proceed to program this goal mentally.

In practice, you will affirm that which is already true about you. The subconscious in turn will simply let you experience it. You will gradually notice a change in feelings and attitudes toward yourself and others. It may take anywhere from one to three weeks before you notice. The growth in this area can be continuous as long as you continue programming it. So make it a lifetime goal.

You have now learned a powerful concept. How well the power works for you will depend on how well you study it, practice it, and live it.

The following relaxation exercise will help you to program your subconscious mind to achieve healthy self-esteem, that vital building block of happiness and success.

Relaxation Exercise for Chapter 7

This relaxation exercise includes affirmations of self-esteem and other general affirmations for attaining your athletic goals.

As you work with these affirmations, practice visualizing each one as you read it or hear it spoken. This will add greatly to the effect of your mental programming. In the future, it may be a good idea to prepare a visualization for each affirmation in advance of doing the relaxation exercise, so that you will be prepared at just the right moment.

☆   ☆   ☆   ☆   ☆

Proceed to relax yourself now in the manner you have learned . . . . . Just close your eyes, settle down in your chair comfortably, loosen any tight or binding clothing, and then begin to lessen surface tension. Take several deep breaths as you have been taught. Sigh them out and feel the relaxing effect as you breathe out the waste air . . . . . Repeat this two or three times . . . . . Then take the next step of remembering relaxation. Remember the most beautiful and deeply that you have ever been relaxed. As you get a mental picture of yourself being completely and totally relaxed, you will also get that nice feeling of relaxation . . . . . .

While you remember that nice feeling, just tell yourself that as you count down from 7 to 1, each number will take you one seventh of the way toward fulfillment of relaxation such as you have just imagined. Just remember how your arms and hands felt . . . . . Remember how your feet and legs felt . . . . . Recall to mind how the whole body felt and how still your mind had become and how good it felt . . . . . You were so relaxed, so serene and tranquil. Imagine yourself that way now and then count down from 7 to 1. Do all this on your own. Proceed now, with the breathing, the imagining, and the counting down from 7 to 1 and bring yourself, on your own, all the way into your scene of nature . . . . . (When complete, proceed.)

You should be just about all the way down to 1 now. You have relaxed yourself, on your own, and have done a splendid job . . . . . Becoming more relaxed all the time. Becoming so relaxed and feeling so serene, so tranquil . . . . . Feel yourself now in that wonderful, quiet state of relaxation . . . . . While you're in this wonderful, peaceful state, let yourself drift to that place in the sun that you have come to know so well . . . . . Feel the warm sun as it melts into your body. Just imagine yourself lying there on your blanket in this beautiful scene of nature . . . . . So relaxed and so still. Looking up into the sky. Seeing that rich, deep blue sky up above with all the little powder puff clouds drifting lazily by . . . .

Assume that feeling of freedom. Be aware of that wonderful feeling that goes with knowing you are a part of the total picture of the world, of the universe. Assume that feeling that comes with liking yourself. That feeling that comes with liking yourself . . . . . and you do like yourself unconditionally. You enjoy being yourself without reservation. You enjoy life. You like life. You value life and you recognize the simple truth that you are life . . . . . Therefore, you value yourself at all times. You like yourself at all times. You enjoy being yourself at all times . . . . . You maintain a very positive self-image at all times and in all circumstances. You maintain a positive view of yourself unceasingly. You maintain a highly positive self-concept in all respects . . . .

You never devalue yourself with self-destructive criticism. You never devalue yourself with self-destructive criticism because you like yourself unconditionally. You deal with every situation in a highly positive and constructive way. You deal with all situations in a highly positive and constructive way . . . . . As you learn the technique of mental mastery, you are also becoming self-governed and self-mastered. As you develop and practice the techniques of mental programming, you find that you are more and more becoming the master of your thoughts, your body, your behavior, and your performance . . . . . You are increasingly in control of yourself. You are increasingly in control of yourself, and this control comes through programming the subconscious mind. Not conscious mind, willpower control, but rather the natural, easy flowing control that comes through intentional use of the subconscious mind . . . .

You enjoy using Mental Dynamics, and therefore you practice goal setting and mental programming as a regular part of your athletic program . . . . . You are growing in confidence and enthusiasm every day, and because of this you always enjoy self-acceptance . . . . . You practice self-acceptance regardless of the rate of progress of your development. You also do this regardless of the success or failure that you experience in competition. You always practice self-acceptance . . . . . You never allow yourself to feel put down because all did not go well. Instead you practice self-acceptance. If there are errors, you note them. You make your corrections, and where appropriate you set new goals. Then you mentally program them . . . . .

You are tapping deeply into the dormant talent and ability within you that you never before realized you possessed. Each and every day you are growing in awareness and understanding that within you is an untapped potential, athletic and otherwise, that you had never before dreamed possible. But now you are grasping this meaning and seek to discover more and more of your capabilities ..... As such, it increasingly feels that you are moving closer to performing at the boundaries of your potential. Yet, you are continuously expanding and pushing out those boundaries ..... Those boundaries are being pushed out further and further. You are enlarging your boundaries of optimal performance ....

And now it is time for you to return to full alertness once again, as you have learned. It is so easy to do. Simply count back slowly from 1 to 7 while telling yourself that each number brings you at least a seventh of the way to full alertness ....

Then when you are all the way back up to 7, take three deep breaths, and on the peak of intake of that third breath you open your eyes, smile, beam, and stretch. Feel alive and alert and refreshed and revitalized, and at the perfect level of consciousness for the next activity that you are to take part in. Proceed now to count back up and take your three deep breaths ....

☆ ☆ ☆ ☆ ☆

Mental Project for Chapter 7

Here is a seven-step project which should lead you to some very interesting conclusions about yourself—and life. Try it and see!

1. Sit for five minutes and quiet your mind and relax your body.
2. Scan your body, from head to toe, with your awareness. See how you feel—tense? loose? nothing?
3. Reflect back briefly in the past to some unhappy interaction between yourself and another person (coach, player, official). Scan your body again. Note any changes; note facial muscles, back, shoulders, and stomach. Are you aware of any tightening, tensing, quickening of breathing, heartbeat or pulse?
4. Now drop that line of thought. Reflect on some person you truly admire, revere, or love.
5. After a few moments of reflection, scan your body again. What happens? Note your facial muscles. Is there a tendency to smile? How do your stomach, shoulders, breathing, and pulse feel? What is the overall effect?
6. Now imagine yourself as being the best person you can be. Perhaps like the one you revere. Imagine really liking yourself—*in any situation*—negative or positive, easy or difficult.
7. Again, scan your body. How does it feel?

Conclusion: Thoughts that are in harmony bring harmonious feelings. When thoughts regarding yourself are in harmony, feelings are right—healthy, happy, and liberating.

You will recognize steps 1, 6, and 7 as parts of the relaxation exercise used to develop a good self-image. These steps should be practiced every day, along with affirmations.

Triple Imagery

As our ability in technique increases, we find that finesse and subtleness start to play the leading role—that mental concentration really becomes the hard work. We learn to project our perfect image before us, so that we can imitate it. As we progress we realize that our limits are mental, and can bind us only so long as we allow them to do so.

JOHN LIND[1]

Now that you know the "secret," you are ready to expand the use of your mental power to achieve even more success. Triple Imagery can lead you to better physical performance and a more creative use of your mind to come up with original solutions to problems that go beyond your immediate physical world. We will talk more of that later in this chapter and give you some specific examples of how this advanced programming works.

We assume you have already applied the techniques of Mental Dynamics that we have described in the previous chapters. With your newly acquired knowledge of goal setting, affirmations, and relaxation exercises, you are ready for Triple Imagery!

Triple Imagery opens yet another dimension to the personal control of your mind, your thoughts, and your progress. Through its use you will be able to program your subconscious more effectively than ever before, allowing you to reinforce and expand on what you have learned up to now. Consider this, if you will, as a graduate course for those who have mastered the previous material, which should now be a regular part of your personal and athletic self-development program.

Triple Imagery is an in-depth relaxation and programming exercise designed to create a state of mental disassociation, a state that so thoroughly involves you in imagery that you lose touch with the here and now. It is called Triple Imagery because you will be able to travel mentally from one imagery to another to another. It is imagery within imagery.

Beginning with your scene of nature, you will be taken to your very own mental training room, a room you will design in your imagination. There you will observe yourself on a view screen. This is a third-person view of

80   [1] Former head coach, Women's Crew Program, University of Washington.

yourself which can be used for perfecting athletic technique or previewing a competitive event.

You will then leave the mental training room to go mentally to your place of physical training or competition. You will experience yourself in the first person, with the same successful actions you just witnessed in the third person on your viewing screen. You had looked into the future, but now you will act out the script as if it were in the present tense.

Since you have seen how you will perform, you now—in the present—actually perform what you know has already happened. You can proceed with confidence and success. The juggling of time and space is all designed to keep you "aloft" and allow for superb programming to take place. The advantage of this type of programming is that it is even more effective than the previous programming exercises you have learned. Master Triple Imagery, and your progress will accelerate.

The Triple Imagery Exercise

The training that you do in your imagination is the same as the real physical training as far as your brain is concerned. In your imagination you can train more perfectly—eliminating errors.

So when you complete your actions in the first person, you return mentally to your scene of nature, and then back to the room where you are doing this exercise, either by memorization, with the help of a friend, or with the use of a tape recorder.

After you become familiar with the process of Triple Imagery, you can do it completely on your own, without the help of friends or a tape recorder. Thus, this technique can be used on site, just a few minutes before actual competition; but it must be mastered first, to be effective.

☆　☆　☆　☆　☆

Carefully and steadily move through all steps of relaxation, on your own, until you are perfectly and deeply relaxed. Use each phase that you have learned: breathing, imagining relaxation, and the 7-to-1 countdown. Then bring yourself, on your own, all the way, deeply into your beautiful scene of nature . . . .

As you mentally project yourself into this passive scene, use all of your senses in order to enjoy and experience it fully. Look around you. See all the beautiful sights. The trees, the ground cover, flowers, whatever there may be. Take it all in and use all of your senses . . . . . Listen, for instance, to the sounds of nature and enjoy them. Hear the sound of water. Perhaps the lapping of water on the beach or the rushing of water in a river . . . . . Use your sense of smell. Enjoy all the beautiful aromas in this place. Completely project yourself into this lovely, quiet scene of nature . . . . . Feel the warmth of the sun on your body. The warmth of the sun which helps you become loose, lazy, languid, and lethargic . . . .

As you stroll along in this beautiful scene, feel yourself becoming completely at one with nature. Feeling so good, so free. Completely free in time and space. Your mind is free to float, to be whatever, wherever, however you wish . . . . . . Finally, as you take in this wonderful scene with all your senses, find a comfortable spot and spread out a blanket and lie down in the sun, or in the shade, whichever you prefer . . . . . .

Just feel so good, so relaxed, so happy inside, so at peace. As you lie here in this wonderful nature scene, allow your eyes to close so that you can no longer see the sky and the trees around you. Rather, allow your mind to construct a very practical room. One that you call your mental training room. Imagine yourself now, approaching this room slowly from the outside. Look at this training room from the outside, in whatever form it may be. Examine the outside walls. Examine the door which you are about to enter. Look it all over very carefully . . . . . . Examine the doorknob if there is one. Now go through the door. Step inside, inspect the room—take in all the details. See everything there is to see . . . . . . Examine the walls. See how they are adorned. Look at the shelves, closets, and pictures. See what they are all made of . . . . . . Look at the ceiling and the floor. Look around at the furniture. Be sure to notice an easy chair, a very comfortable easy chair . . . . . Notice that directly across the room from your chair is a large viewing screen approximately 6 by 8 feet in size. That is the screen on which you will view your athletic performance and techniques. You will be able to watch yourself in training or in competitive action . . . . . .

Adjoining the arm of your easy chair is an adjustable control panel that is available to you as you sit in your chair. Try it out. Just take a seat in your easy chair, lean back, and then swing the adjustable control panel into position. Now it is comfortably located in front of you, and you can inspect it . . . . . . Notice the various knobs, buttons, and dials . . . . . . Notice one set of controls that manipulates time . . . . . . A clock that goes forward, another that goes backward. A calendar that moves days and weeks and months ahead, and another one that moves backward . . . . . . You are able to turn time forward or backward and can use the screen to view events that have already happened, and some that have yet to happen . . . . . . You can review, analyze, or revivicate past performances by turning the clock back. You can project future performances by turning the clock ahead. You will be able to see anything that you need to see. There are other switches and controls. Switches to start films. Switches to dim lights. Others for sounds. But for now, just turn on the "on" or power switch of your viewing equipment . . . . .

You will project onto the screen a picture of yourself. You will be able to watch yourself now in training. If you prefer, you can watch yourself performing in competition, if you have a specific event coming up. You have a choice. You can see anything you wish to see. Pick one or the other. Training or performance. The time that you will be watching is fifteen minutes into the future. You are about to view yourself as you will actually be doing in a few minutes. You observe yourself now preparing for the act of practice or competitive performance. Thus, see yourself on the screen, getting ready. View yourself getting ready mentally to do what you are about to do. See yourself on that screen assuming an ideal mental state of readiness, including confidence and relaxed concentration. See the look of knowing that whatever you set out to do you can do . . . . . . Now observe yourself as you begin your motions and movements. As you practice or perform, observe yourself in whatever technique is relevant to your sport . . . . . . This may include offensive and/or defensive actions. It includes any kind of technique that is of interest and importance to you at this time . . . .

If you use equipment in your sport, observe yourself on that screen as being in total harmony with this equipment. In total harmony with your use of it . . . . . See yourself in harmony with the task before you, and with the equipment. Notice the precision with which you move. Notice the efficient and effective movement. Every movement appropriate to the task at hand. Every movement executed with exactly the perfect amount of energy that's needed to perform it. Not too much, not too little. Just the right amount . . . . . .

Notice, as you observe yourself on the screen, how adaptable and adjustable you are to all unexpected situations and conditions that arise. On your screen observe these conditions arising, and watch yourself as you make your remarkable corrections and adjustments.

Depending on whether your technique and performance call for strength, endurance, or finesse, see yourself working with all the strength, endurance, or finesse required for your sport . . . . . .

Notice the concentration on your face. Notice the perfect coordination. Notice the successful fulfillment of your goal, whether it be in training or competition. See how successful you are with what you set out to do. See the evidence on your screen . . . . . .

You have enjoyed watching yourself on the screen and you have been impressed with what you have accomplished. Now remember again that you have been viewing yourself as you will perform, in just a few minutes. So now you arise from your chair and leave your mental training room. Step outside, where you find yourself actually at the scene that you have just viewed. You are actually at the arena, the court, the field, where you will actually train and compete. Create this scene as it will be. You may find either a practice place or the scene of actual competition. Whichever it is, it will be the same as you have just witnessed on the screen. Now you will perform exactly what you saw. For what you saw was a projection into the future. When you viewed yourself, you saw what you are now about to do. So now you can go about it with complete and total confidence, for you know how it will turn out. So now you are preparing yourself for this practice or competitive performance. Now you are getting ready, physically warming up and mentally warming up. Just as you saw yourself do on the screen. You are preparing yourself physically and mentally. Feel the feelings that come with being ready physically, mentally, and emotionally ...... Assume the very idea of mental readiness. Especially that of supreme confidence, relaxed concentration. Set your attitude of great confidence, and a feeling of knowing .....

Now you're ready to proceed with your moves and actions. Whatever it is that you are doing, proceed with your special technique. Offensive or defensive moves, or whatever else is significant or important ..... Proceed with feeling totally in harmony with your equipment and with the task you are performing. Feel the wonderful feeling that occurs when you know you're doing things right ...... Feel your efficiency, your precision, and your effectiveness. Every movement, effective and efficient. Every movement a correct movement ......

Notice things happening that you hadn't planned on. Perhaps a strong gust of wind. A change in other conditions, air temperature, precipitation, or unexpected moves on the part of someone else. Notice how adaptable you are. Feel how quickly you adjust. How flexible you are physically and mentally. Nothing is disturbing you. You are enjoying every change. You're enjoying adjusting to all situations and conditions ......

Feel the strength that comes surging from you. Notice your endurance and finesse. Feel the satisfaction of every fine movement. Experience the success of what you're doing. Feel the feelings in your body of what you're doing ......

Now as you complete what you are doing, see yourself totally 100 percent successful in fulfilling the goal of this particular activity, whether it be practice or competition.

Now return in consciousness, easily, gradually, to your scene of nature ...... Then move from the scene of nature. Bring your consciousness back from the sounds, aromas, and feelings of the nature around you. Remove the feelings of this warm sun. Remove the sights and bring your consciousness back to the place where you are conducting this exercise .....

To return yourself to full alertness, simply use the methods you were taught earlier. Count back up from 1 to 7. Tell yourself that each number brings you a seventh of the way back. Then take three deep breaths as you recall. This will bring you to a level that is appropriate and right for whatever it is you are to do next . . . . . .

☆ ☆ ☆ ☆ ☆

Just as you would naturally take time to train for your sport through physical conditioning programs and game practice sessions, so also is it important to include Triple Imagery in your training schedule. It is the kind of exercise that leads to increasingly improved results when practiced on a regular basis, because, in addition to the regular mental programming benefits achieved, it can serve you well for other special projects in other areas of life.

For example, Jim Miller, a national powerboat champion and holder of the world's speed record in his Pro-1100 CC Runabout class, used his mental training room to develop a new mystery engine.

He raced for several years with equipment that he regarded as very average. Miller was unable to place much better than second in competition. Through experience and mental programming, he knew that he should be a first-place racer but was limited by his equipment.

So he purchased a new boat. But to be certain he would have the best equipment possible, Jim spent many hours in his mental training room designing, building, and testing the newest, hottest engine available.

He called it his "Mystery Engine." He then began actual construction of the engine. This involved casting some parts, machining others, and bringing together what he considered the best parts available from several manufacturers of outboard equipment. As he proceeded, he used his mental training room to plan his moves, and little by little all the pieces fell into place.

After 250 hours of building this engine it was ready for testing and showed real promise. But because of some too-tight clearances, it had to be repaired and tried again the following week.

This time, everything went perfectly. The outfit ran seven miles per hour faster than any previous combination of boat and engine, and in September 1978, Miller established a new five-mile APBA World Speed Record for his class of boat.

Your use of Triple Imagery can be very flexible. Feel free to stretch your imagination or use gimmicks. After all, you are working with your subconscious mind and it seems to enjoy novel approaches.

Bill Griffith, when in his mental training room, would sometimes imagine there was a mechanical track, under the raging river, which followed along the slalom course on which he paddled his canoe. He then imagined his boat attached to a motorized device which could pull his boat along the zigzag course, upstream, downstream, forward, and backward at speeds that his conscious mind could not accept if he were to do it unaided.

Thus he grew accustomed to seeing himself moving at speeds unthinkable by normal standards. It worked for Bill as he moved up in the competition and in 1975 placed sixth in world championshp canoe slalom competition in Skopje, Yugoslavia.

Riley Moss also stretched his imagination as he viewed himself on the screen of his mental training room.

Riley, an avid mountain climber, delighted in solo climbs and would often challenge peaks and walls that others shunned. To refine his skill, he would often see himself on his viewing screen and very carefully attend to all details of climbing skills.

To make sure he had a complete perspective, he sometimes imagined the picture on the screen as coming from a camera placed in a helicopter which could move around from one side view to another, plus take shots from above and below. He was thus able to view his climbing technique from every conceivable angle, which in turn led to actual improved skill. To this day many of his friends still shake their heads over his conquests.

When you use your Triple Imagery, remember to let yourself go. Use your imagination fully. It will serve you well.

Mental Project for Chapter 8

During one of your relaxation sessions, try this exercise, which will profoundly impact your awareness of the extent of the power the subconscious has over your body.

Sit in an easy chair where your arm can hang over the sides comfortably for a length of time.

Close your eyes, and when you have established a *deep* level of relaxation, while retaining control over your thinking, analytical mind, tell yourself, and visualize it as well, that on the right side of your chair there is a bucket of water that slowly but surely is getting warmer and warmer. Even imagine it sitting on a stove with a hot fire underneath. Then mentally place your hand in the bucket of warm water. Physically you may actually lift your arm and hand as you visualize placing your hand in the bucket of *warm, warm* water. Keep reminding yourself of the gradually increasing warmth until you can feel your hand actually getting warm.

Persist with imagery and suggestion and soon you will notice even more warmth in your hand. Continue to make it warmer.

After you have accomplished the warming in your right hand, repeat the same process with the left hand. Only this time, imagine the water as *cold, cold, cold.* Imagine a cold bucket full of ice chunks and *feel* your hand getting colder. Feel the fingers getting stiff and numb.

Now imagine both water buckets and both hands as growing more and more uncomfortable from the cold or hot water. *Keep this up until you can feel each hand as hot and cold.*

Now, for some additional fun, slowly raise your cold hand and touch your face with it and visualize the coldness running out of your fingers onto your cheeks. Gently rub your fingers on both sides of your face and continue to imagine the coldness of your fingers going into your face with the result that your cheeks become cold and numb. Tell yourself that muscle control is reduced or eliminated as if you had had an anesthetic. Touch your lips and tongue and let the numbness and stiffness take over there. After a few minutes, try talking or working your mouth and you will be amazed to see how effective you have been.

Once you have completed this portion of the exercise to your satisfaction, proceed to the next stage by taking your warm hand and rubbing your face wherever it was numb. Imagine the warmth flowing from your fingers into the facial muscles and flesh, causing them to feel normal and good once again. When that is completed, rub your hands together and let the warmth of one hand warm the other and allow the coolness of the other to cool the first until both hands return to their normal state.

Once this has been accomplished, take advantage of your relaxed state to proceed with other projects, such as mental programming of goals, or complete the relaxation exercise and return once again to full alertness.

The results of this exercise may vary, especially on your first attempt. Some will experience all that was described very noticeably, some less so. Also, some of the time you may do very well, some of the time less so, but *with practice*, you can master it.

Once you are able to make this work, and can see clearly how powerful and subtle your mind really is, you can vary your objectives. For example, using similar techniques, imagine greater reserves of strength, power, finesse, or endurance. Practice any *special need* you may have in this way and then see how your subconscious can help bring it about.

9 Energy Flow

He [the oriental] is taught from childhood that there are many
subtle forces and forms of energy in nature, which may be taken
advantage of and pressed into service by Man.

YOGI RAMACHARAKA[1]

Energy Flow is a relaxation exercise that combines several techniques: suggestion, imagery, breathing, and yoga. The name of the exercise comes from the
imagery used to accomplish its goals.

This is a most potent exercise, remarkable for its numerous benefits. It
may be used as a mental elixir for physical revitalization, reenergizing, pain
management, acceleration of nature's repair power, mental and physical
relaxation, and for warming extremities such as the hands and feet. When
fully relaxed with the Energy Flow technique, it is also a good time for
meditation or mental programming. For most people it is a mental tonic, and
for some it is a spiritual experience.

This exercise, like the others, must be practiced to gain greatest profici-
ency and ease of use. Eventually you can use it throughout the entire body at
one time, or specifically at just one part for purposes of pain relief or quickening of natural repair.

Though unusual in name and practice, this relaxation exercise can be a
most remarkable experience and one well worth perfecting. You should find
much pleasure and benefit from its use.

The Energy Flow Exercise

Place yourself so that you are seated comfortably in your chair with your feet
flat on the floor and your hands apart, either on your lap or on the arms of
the chair. Be sure that your clothing is loose and not binding.

☆　☆　☆　☆　☆

90　　[1] *Science of Psychic Healing* (Des Plaines, IL: Yoga Publication Society, 1934).

With your eyes closed, consider the room you are in. Imagine the room as gradually filling up with a soft misty fog. Visualize this expanding fog in whatever way is natural and comfortable for you. Let your imagination run free and allow this mist to come from any source that you wish. It could be like the mist from a steam room or like a cloud bank rolling in through the window. Give it a hint of color, if you wish, or a pleasant aroma. Imagine this mist becoming thicker and thicker, and feel the room filling up in such a way that it is barely possible to see across it. Let your imagination run even freer by accepting the fact that this energy mist is actually a very special magical substance; a substance that can be directed to flow in a manner that will help you in many, many special ways. It is especially good for relaxing the whole body or, if you wish, only specific parts of the body. It is good for the management and control of pain, as well as discomfort and tension. This Energy Flow can also be used for healing purposes. It is a technique for accelerating the healing processes that are natural to the body. It is also effective for eliminating headaches and other tension-caused body aches. Energy Flow is a superb tonic and can be of great benefit while revitalizing and reenergizing the body. It has special favor to those who would like to use it to feel the surge and increase of self-confidence that is available through this technique. It can be used in such a manner that it restores self-confidence quickly.

As you have filled your space with this mist, you will begin to breathe it in. First, we would like you to take a couple of deep breaths of this imaginary mist, just to get it into your system. Take a couple of deep breaths and remember as you exhale that only the waste air is being breathed out. Special qualities of the energy mist remain with the body and are now circulating throughout. On the next breath you take, push a little harder and force some of the mist—that energizing mist—up to your shoulders. Then over to your dominant arm and finally all the way down to your dominant hand. If you are right-handed, your right hand will be your dominant hand. Push the mist all the way down to your hand as you inhale. Give that push and imagine that the mist is flowing down your arm into your hand. With your mind, direct the mist to your hand until such time as you can feel the hand relax, tingle, or until it becomes warm. At that point, continue to direct more energy to the hand in this same manner. Just continue visualizing the energy and the mist directed to the hand, and let the relaxing or warmth happen as a result. *Do not try to force it.*

Now continue on with that . . . . . . Warm the hand some more so that it becomes warmer or hotter . . . . . Some achieve this in less than thirty seconds; others may require several minutes . . . . . . Now visualize the mist flowing into your lower arm in the same fashion . . . . . Now that you have the lower arm full of this flowing energy, you will find that it will continue to flow on into your hand and the arm even as we progress into other parts of the body . . . .

Now continue by saturating your elbow area with this mist. Then go all the way up the arm until you are satisfied that the arm is all done . . . . . Every now and then take another special breath of the mist so as to increase the effect. As you do so, as you saturate the body with this energy mist, you may become impressed with the fact that different parts of the body appear unusually warm. Some parts will seem less affected than others. Some parts more than the others. Frequently, we find that the warmth tends to concentrate in those areas of the body that have been injured previously, such as old scar tissue and broken bones. If there is some area of the body that is now tense, or injured, you may find that this warm energy surrounds it and takes the pain and discomfort away . . . .

Proceed now to the other hand and arm. Start with the hand and direct the flow of energy mist to it, just as you did on the first side. When you feel the results, just continue directing the Energy Flow to it until it is time to move on. Do you feel the hand starting to tingle just a little bit? Are you getting some warmth in it? Continue giving it a little bit more and then proceed up the arm, the elbow, all the way to the upper arm. When you get all the way up to the shoulder, pause once again and repeat for reinforcement and deepening. Until you feel it is time to move on. Very good . . . .

One wonderful feature of this Energy Flow is that it can revitalize and reenergize the body. On those occasions when you are feeling tired from lack of rest or extra exertion, you will find that this Energy Flow has the power and properties of giving you renewed energy, strength, and vitality. As you open your eyes from the experience, you will notice this in yourself . . . .

Now take another breath of this energy mist and visualize it flowing from your lungs up to both the right and left shoulders and in front and in back. Feel those shoulders and all the muscles filling up with the energy. Take your time. Fill them up with energy and let them relax. Then as you accomplish that, move down to the chest area. Fill the muscles of the chest with this mist, both inside and out. Let the energy flow. Just feel the body relaxing as you do this. Enjoy the wonderful feeling that comes from this exercise . . . .

Now move on to the stomach area. Direct the energy to all the muscles of the stomach outside and then to all the organs inside of the upper abdomen. Imagine this energy just soaking in, saturating all the cells, tissues, muscles, and organs and causing them perfect health—causing them to function perfectly at all times . . . .

Now identify the region just at the base of the sternum, or breastbone, just a little beneath the rib cage and above the navel. Take a breath and then direct this mist directly to that area. Imagine the energy flowing all the way through to the backbone and into the region called the solar plexus. Fill that area. Saturate it with the mist. Concentrate on that for a while and allow yourself to enjoy whatever experience results from it . . . . Now move down to the lower abdomen and repeat the process again. Take another breath of the energy mist and then direct its flow to the lower regions. To all the muscles and organs. Saturate them . . . . . When you have completed that part of the assignment, let yourself feel, sense, and enjoy the Energy Flow . . . .

Now be aware of both thighs, the knees, calves, and the feet as you direct the mist to these regions. Just imagine the mist flowing through your thighs and into the calves as it works its way down to the feet. It does its work as it flows through the legs, so that all the muscles are being relaxed as that energy flows all the way down to the feet and toes. When you get this energy all the way to the feet and toes and you can feel them warming and tingling, just pause a little bit, reinforce the treatment further, and let yourself enjoy it . . . .

If you're having any difficulty achieving this effect with the feet, try wiggling the toes a little bit at first, so that you can focus your awareness on them . . . . . Notice the feet beginning to warm up. Give them another charge of energy. See if you can get them nice and warm . . . .

Then direct your awareness to the other end of your body, to the back of the neck, and mentally cause the energy to flow there. Let it flow back and forth and all around the neck at the base of the skull—gradually from side to side . . . . . Push the energy down through all the muscles of the back, starting at the shoulders. Work your way from side to side. Let this energy flow back and forth saturating all the back muscles all the way down to the hips . . . . . When you complete that, come back up to the base of the skull. Be aware of the spinal column. Cause the misty energy to flow all around the spinal column. From the base of the skull up and down, all the way to the tailbone. Let this energy soak into the spinal column—that bale of wires that is transmitting signals to every part of the body. Saturate the spinal column with energy. Imagine it fanning out, flowing throughout your whole body via this wiring of the nervous system, just like it is in a telegraph circuit. Feel your whole body becoming like light, becoming more electric, more alive. It is completely relaxed, yet beautifully alive, with this energy flowing through the human telegraph system. All over your body at once. Almost a light—electrifying! . . . .

Very gradually now bring your awareness up to the back of your head. Direct this energy mist to the back of your head, up and across the top of the head. All the way until you get to the forehead region. Be sure to take care of the sides as well. Direct the mist up there. Imagine it just soaking into the brain . . . .

Finally with another deep breath, give a good push, and imagine that energy flowing all the way up the spinal column, across the head, and to that region above the eyes in the middle between the brows. Focus all the mist in that center area of the head. Feel the flow of that energy as it travels up your spinal column into the forehead region. Then feel the peace that comes from that. A sense of tranquillity, confidence, self-assurance, and power. Enjoy the sensations that come from this procedure, and then repeat that Energy Flow deep breath as just described—one more time . . . .

If any part of your body is tight, tense, uncomfortable, in pain, disabled, or diseased, direct the Energy Flow to that part of the body and give it a heavy dose.

If you would like to do some mental programming of goals at this time, just pause a moment and take advantage of the "good feeling" and relaxed condition you have created. Use the appropriate affirmations and visualizations to program the desired goals. This is a good time to see yourself operating in all that you do in a very effective, efficient, challenging, interesting way—yet always in control. Always in charge: self-governed, self-directed, self-mastered. Always enjoying everything you do. See yourself as a person who enjoys everything you undertake. Every situation that in the past might have been a problem to you is now seen as a welcome challenge. An opportunity to test yourself, to grow, and to expand. See yourself in all your activities as a person in command, in charge, relaxed, busy, active, successful, decisive. All the qualities that you deem important, and yet displaying those qualities in a relaxed, easygoing, effective way.

When you are through with all of your programming, and wish to end your Energy Flow relaxation exercise, just take three deep breaths and on the peak of intake of that third breath, open your eyes, feel reenergized, revitalized, relaxed, alert, and in tune with life.

☆   ☆   ☆   ☆   ☆

Mental Project for Chapter 9

A principle well worth memorizing is the psychological law of reversed effect. This law says that when the will and the imagination are in conflict, the imagination usually triumphs. In other words, it is not uncommon for people to exercise great amounts of willpower—I will not smoke, I will not smoke, I *WILL* not smoke!—while at the same time imagining exactly the opposite. While declaring that they will not smoke, they actually imagine picking up a cigarette and lighting it, and this imagining, though often subtle, is enough to cause more smoking behavior. The imagination prevails over the will. And so, although it is essential to use your will for such activity as selecting your goals and persisting in them, it is even more important, once "will" has been put into effect, to back off—and let your imagination have full sway. Let yourself imagine the goal accomplished. To experience this point, try taking a seat and relax yourself. Clasp your hands together with fingers interlaced as you might do in prayer or contemplation.

Then imagine those hands completely glued together. Imagine the fingers are locked, the muscles rigid, and in no way will the hands separate. Now if you will continue to *keep that image* in your mind, proceed next with all the will you can muster to tell yourself (will yourself) to pull the hands apart. With all your might, *TRY, TRY, TRY,* to pull the hands apart while continuing to imagine them locked together.

If your imagination is complete enough, you will discover that no matter how hard you will or try, it is to no avail. When you stop *willing* and just *imagine* the fingers relaxing, they will slip gently apart.

Now you can see that as important as will is, the imagination can be even more powerful in control of the body. Instead of using willpower to control actions, use it to define the goal and to direct and sustain the picture of the goal.

10 Guardians of the Mind

Perfection is not attained at that point at which nothing else can be added, but at that point at which nothing else can be taken away.

CHARLES ("BUD") WILKINSON[1]

Because of some negative lifetime habits of thinking, people are in a continuous effort of holding on to the control of their thinking minds. The subconscious mind is sensitive and responsive to self-generated negative thoughts as well as those from the outside environment.

Therefore, another step in learning to control our lives is to increase the understanding of the process of the mind, and how it is influenced by our own random thoughts and the impact of our environment. We will first consider two new, and similar, techniques called "monitoring" and "filtering," which are aptly called the "guardians of the mind." Later in this chapter we will also discuss revivication, sometimes called the "editor" of our thoughts.

MONITORING

Monitoring is the method we use to gain control over the quality of thought that we ourselves may allow to influence our subconscious. Monitoring allows us to detect errors in thinking (negative input). Once detected, these faults are then automatically corrected.

By now you know we believe very strongly that mental programming, with affirmations and imagery, is really great for achieving goals and changing your life for the better. It is well established and has been proven beyond any doubt that it works. And it works well!

And yet there are some people who claim that affirmations don't work at all, no matter how hard they try. Others occasionally complain that the system works too slowly. Even some of the more ardent supporters of our

98   [1] Frank Litsky, *Superstars* (Secaucus, N.J.: Derbibooks, Inc., 1975).

mental techniques will occasionally state that the system works well for some goals, but fails for others. Why is this? If affirmations are really supposed to be so great, why aren't they always working? How is it possible to make them work consistently? That is the key question of this chapter.

Here's an example of the type of problem that monitoring is designed to eliminate: Recently a woman gymnast complained to us that although she had been studying mental programming techniques, mind development, mind control, and related studies for several years, they just didn't work for her. She was very adamant about the failure of these techniques to work for her. As she continued to talk, we noticed something in her discussion that struck a responsive chord. She had been repeating the thought that mental programming didn't work for so many months and years that that idea had become the dominant thought in her subconscious mind. That thought had become a successful affirmation, which said, in effect, that her athletic goals and programming efforts would not work. She had been successfully affirming that her other affirmations would fail! And, in fact, that one affirmation was succeeding remarkably well.

She was also frequently guilty of negating other goals. She would say, "I can't stay on my training schedule." Or "It's hard to learn that new technique." Plus a whole string of other negatives, which included, "I just can't communicate with others very well .... I know I'll never learn that defensive position.... I'm always losing my temper .... Nothing I ever do is right—I'm just a hopeless case." These are extreme remarks and can have a devastating effect on efforts to better oneself.

This, unfortunately, is a rather frequent example of how people unconsciously affirm the failure of their goals.

Before we look further at monitoring, let's review our understanding of the mind, which will help to explain the process of monitoring and how it will help you. You have learned much about the mind and the part that thought plays in shaping and influencing the mind, and especially in programming it for the long range. To be influenced by thought is usually a "now" experience. That is, thought can cause a person to feel, think, or act right now—in a very short time span. But thought also *programs* the mind and can therefore have a long-range effect on a person. Remembering this fact will help you to understand how monitoring is an important part of your goal of being a self-governed and self-directed person.

Thought comes to us from both ourselves and the environment. Further on in this chapter we will discuss the management of thoughts that come to us from the environment, a technique called "filtering." For now, however, we will continue to focus on monitoring, which is *a technique for dealing with our own thoughts and making certain that only the right thoughts— those that are harmonious with our goals—are being used.*

We know that when positive thoughts are introduced to the subconscious, they can lift and renew us, and cause us to be a more positive person. We experience greater positive output in the form of positive feelings, actions, and thoughts. We also know that when negative thoughts are introduced there is a tendency for those thoughts to have a negative effect, leading to a greater negative output in the form of negative feelings, actions, and thoughts.

You are now practicing positive input through your recently learned mental programming techniques. You use affirmation and visualization. And through those techniques you introduce positive goals into your mental computer. And so, if you have a greater abundance of positive thoughts outweighing the negative thoughts relative to a specific goal, it's obvious that the positive will be the dominating force. However, it is not unusual to find a person, such as the gymnast we described earlier, who does his or her affirmations and visualizations and then comes to us and says, "These things don't work. Nothing seems to be happening."

After reviewing all the circumstances we inevitably come to the conclusion that the system works, that thoughts do determine reality; but the fact is, such a person's goals are not being achieved because of one common error: *The wrong dominant thought is still in control*! And even though he or she may be doing affirmations and visualizing a certain goal, the dominant thought remains counter to that goal. In short, these people practice what we sometimes refer to as the *negation ratio*. They may practice a 25 to 1 ratio. Some people even establish a 50 to 1 ratio. This means that for every one positive affirmation the individual repeats, he or she manages to use at least twenty-five or fifty negative thoughts relative to that goal. This becomes such a routine habit that the person is usually not consciously aware that all this is going on.

It's important to remember that affirmations, or even verbalized thoughts, often trigger visualizations. So when we negate verbally we may trigger a negative visualization. As an example, athletes attempting to lose weight for training purposes will affirm that they will lose so many pounds. And yet, when they finish their affirming they go about the day talking to their friends about weight control and *how difficult it is*. They continually refer to how heavy they are and how hard it is to stay on a training diet. And before they know it, in the course of a day, these people have logged at least fifty negative statements about themselves and weight control.

For some people, a high negation ratio relates to almost everything they do. These are very failure-prone people. But for most of us, high negation ratios only occur in certain selected areas, sports activities being a prime example. Most of your goals are likely being realized just fine, but there may be a couple that you are having trouble with. That's where monitoring comes to the rescue. It is essential to detect these negations before they become firmly planted in the subconscious.

In computer language a monitor is a circuit system that is so programmed that it alerts the operator whenever an error occurs. This monitor circuit can even provide the suggested correction to the error. Since our subconscious is so much like a computer, this method works effectively for us as well.

This is how your monitor will work once you have established it: Anytime your thoughts run contrary to your declared goals, the subconscious will alert you, just as if a bell or buzzer were to go off to let you know that something is amiss. Some people seem naturally to have this kind of built-in monitor. Other people have to learn it or program it. But it is a very effective and helpful tool. How does it work? Well, it's basically very simple. Once the monitor, which you have affirmed into existence, is established, it alerts you to negative data. It somehow creates an expanded awareness in your mind for certain kinds of thoughts.

But the monitoring process does not end there. It is not enough to identify the error of thought; you must also eliminate this error. You must correct it. Once you detect the negative input, it is *essential* to correct it. You must go a step further and make the corrective change. This in essence is the simplest part of monitoring and is perhaps the most important part of all.

And so, if you detect thoughts of a self-devaluing nature, you must correct them immediately, in the form of an affirmation. If you hear yourself saying, "I hope the hitter doesn't hit a grounder to me now because I usually muff grounders in key situations," then catch this negative thought in the making, and correct it with a positive affirmation, such as, "I always play better in clutch situations. I hope he hits it right to *me!*"

Never allow yourself to say that something is hard or tough. If you ever hear yourself saying that something is difficult or contrary to your goal, make the appropriate correction immediately. In a very short time you will notice that the negative thoughts no longer get fully formed before your monitoring circuit cuts them off and replaces them with positive inputs.

This monitoring technique is a truly effective tool, and we have seen it work beautifully in hundreds of cases. One weekend tennis player we know used it to great advantage in improving his game and his attitude. An average player at best, he was impatient with his results and seemed to feel that he should play better. Unconsciously he began to berate himself by making such statements as, "You should have gotten that point. You can do better than that, you dummy. I always hit backhand volleys on the frame." And so on, through each weekend, until he began to develop fits of temper and racquet throwing. The latter, of course, only tended to reinforce his poor opinion of himself, and were the physical manifestation of his frustration in failing to meet the desired goals of his game. Of course, you are now aware of the negative affirmations that were at play for this man. Those affirmations were working wonderously well, but that poor hacker wasn't even aware of what he was doing to his mental game.

Later, this man became aware of the techniques of mental dynamics used in this book. One of his goals was to set up a monitor. Within a couple of weeks he was able to eliminate nearly all negative thoughts while playing. He no longer criticized himself for missed shots. Instead, he would mentally, and verbally, recite a positive affirmation, and look forward eagerly to an opportunity to play another shot just like the one he had missed—because he *knew* he was going to perform it correctly next time. And more often than not, he did!

Within a month this man was playing a higher level of tennis and was enjoying it more than ever before. His tennis-playing friends were amazed by his change in results and court deportment.

Here's another way to think about monitoring: Hypnotize yourself with the thoughts you want to be hypnotized with, instead of parroting old ideas and clichés. *Learn to think the way you wish to experience life and learn not to think what you do not wish to experience.* You can think the way you wish to experience life with the help of this monitor system. All you have to do is to affirm to yourself as follows: "I HAVE A MONITOR SYSTEM THAT ALERTS ME TO ANY AND ALL THOUGHTS AND IDEAS NOT IN HARMONY WITH MY HEALTH, WELFARE, OR GOALS, ESPECIALLY MY GOAL OF BEING_____."

You will find that the subconscious will take this monitor idea and set it up for you immediately in your mental computer. It will happen automatically, when you have processed it through the subconscious mind. It will work just as it did when you were a student in school. For example, a monitor may have been established so that when you gave a verbal report you soon learned not to say "and—uh." Perhaps you can remember when it was pointed out to you that you were doing this. It surprised you because you didn't realize how many times you were saying "and—uh" until someone told you that you had repeated "and—uh" at least seventy-two times. Then the next time you gave your report, you could hear the "and-uh" even before it came out of your mouth. Little by little you cut down, until eventually you were able to eliminate almost all of the unwanted "and—uhs."

The same principle works with the monitor we are discussing here. Determine in advance what you wish to monitor and then, as we said before, affirm to your subconscious, "I have a monitor system that alerts me to any and all thoughts and ideas not in harmony with my health, welfare, or goals, especially my goal of being_____."

In summary, a monitor is a mental system that we can program into our minds, through affirmation, which alerts us to negative inputs and allows us to change those thoughts to positive inputs for our subconscious.

Now let us consider another mental programming system, filtering.

FILTERING

A filter is similar in concept to a monitor, except that a filter system is one that screens out all ideas and thoughts that are counter to your health, welfare, and goals when they come to you from the environment rather than from within the mind. This outside environment includes other people, newspapers, books, television, radio, movies, and all other forms of communication. Sometimes it may be from teammates and even coaches.

In the case of monitoring, we were able to control our own minds. However, we can seldom control what others do and think, so we need to filter their inputs, rather than attempt to monitor them.

Too many well-meaning people—and sometimes not so well meaning—will come to you and say, "It's awfully tough to do what you're planning. I don't think it will work, so why waste your time?" Or "You'll never make the team, why don't you give it up?" Such comments must be automatically filtered, and you must affirm that the person who said them just doesn't understand the situation. You must reject such inputs continuously and not allow those thoughts to have any effect on your subconscious mind.

We must recognize that the negative thoughts of others can affect us, discourage us, bring us down, and otherwise alter the positive mental posture we are striving to establish and maintain. And above all else, we must remember that these continued contrary inputs can have a long-range programming effect that will often negate all our attempts at positive programming.

Therefore, filtering has been developed as a mental method for neutralizing environmentally originated thoughts that are counter to, or in disharmony with, your declared goals and aspirations.

This type of filtering system allows for the passage of only useful and helpful elements of thought to that important destination—the subconscious.

You probably remember times when you were excited about a plan to change some aspect of your life for the better. You probably told your friends and relatives about your plan, fully expecting them to share your enthusiasm. But what they responded with was, "You're going to what?" And human nature being what it is, they likely brought forth all the reasons why *they* thought your idea would not work. After their bombardment of negatives, you may have abandoned your dreams, simply because you did not have a filter.

Another place where filtering is especially useful is in combating psyching by opponents. Like the tennis player who watches his opponent warm up and then mentions casually, "Your backhand looks a little off today." Or the miler who reminds another runner, "Be careful in the north turn; that's where you fell last year." These types of comments can be completely neutralized by a properly affirmed filter.

On the other hand, filtering should never be construed as a device to cause the proverbial deaf ear. It should not cause one to ignore criticism or suggestions, many of which will be valid and helpful. It simply keeps the control and power of your mind where it belongs—with you.

This filter is easily established by presenting to the subconscious your wish that it exists. Affirm your filter, along with your other affirmations, as follows: "I HAVE AN EFFECTIVE FILTER SYSTEM THAT ELIMINATES THE DESTRUCTIVE EFFECT OF ALL THOUGHTS RECEIVED THAT ARE COUNTER TO MY HEALTH, WELFARE, OR GOALS."

Use this affirmation regularly until you observe that what others say, do, and think no longer has any power over you.

With the conscious introduction of monitoring and filtering affirmations to your subconscious, you will soon be aware that negatives no longer adversely impact your life. You will find yourself moving steadily toward effective realization of your dreams and goals, and toward a wonderfully growing sense of *self-mastery*.

REVIVICATION

Webster defines revivication as "the process of getting new life and vigor." We prefer to think of it as "editing the film." It is a technique by which we can revise and correct certain data stored in the memory bank of our mental computers. If an error has occurred in your daily behavioral experience, and you wish to correct that error for the benefit of your memory bank—in order to have the computer programmed for more perfect performance in the future—you can employ revivication. It can be used in several ways. For one, it is a technique used successfully by people who have injured themselves. For example, after a broken leg is set and placed in a cast, revivication can be used to eliminate or minimize the pain associated with the accident. The victim can start this process by simply sitting in a chair with his eyes closed. Then, after first relaxing himself, he will mentally replay or reimagine the accident scene. He will do this from a few seconds before the accident all the way through to a few seconds after the accident. But he only does this once with the original sensory inputs and feelings. He then repeats the sequence several times, making changes each time. During each repetition he will change the scene or "edit the film." He will change the picture so that it shows him having less and less pain associated with the accident. It will show him being injured, but with the pain occurring in such a way that it is barely noticeable. Strange as it may seem, upon completing this editing process three or four times, the patient will open his eyes and discover—to his delight—that much of the pain has left him. (This technique is explained in more detail in other books.)

This same principle can be used by athletes who have learned to prepare themselves mentally for their particular sporting event. Revivication is a way to correct physical as well as mental errors in the pursuit of sporting excellence. If an error is made, it can be corrected by sitting down quietly, eyes closed, and then replaying or revivicating the sequence. The athlete will imagine himself in that sequence, once again, from a few seconds before the error occurred until a few seconds afterward. Each time he relives it, he will make a correction, until at last he is replaying the scene as it should have been. Then he will repeat that successful scene several times, reinforcing it in his own computer mind—the subconscious. In this way, he has made a correction in his brain tissue, as it were, *so that he will be storing the corrected version of the event in memory, rather than retaining the incorrect version.* That which is stored, of course, influences future behavior and athletic performance.

So if at any time you have performed poorly, or have fallen into bad habits, or because you have not practiced Mental Dynamics consistently, or have allowed yourself too many counterproductive thoughts, then make the correction as soon as possible. Sit down and employ the technique of revivication. This means close your eyes and *replay the scene the way you would have preferred it to happen.* Replay the scene so it is in harmony with the performance and consciousness of a winning athlete!

Use this technique and you will find that it helps you in the days to come. Remember to repeat your scene a number of times, each time making it more perfect, editing it until you can visualize that scene as a great performance. In this way, you will be reprogramming your subconscious to eliminate negative inputs and to lead you to more perfect results the next time you compete.

In summary, remember these important guardians of the mind: monitoring, filtering, and revivication. These are your helpers that increase the potential of your programmed goals by warding off, and rendering harmless, the opponent—negative thought. Develop each guardian through practice until you experience it working on your behalf. Remember, in many sports the key to a good offense is a good defense. Monitoring, filtering, and revivication are your defensive team.

Here is a review of your team:

1. Monitoring allows you to control the quality of thought you yourself may allow to influence your subconscious.
2. Filtering is a system that screens out negative thoughts that come to you from the environment around you.
3. Revivication allows you to "edit the film," to correct certain data stored in your mental computer, so that only positive images remain.

11 Creative Mental Programming

The human mind should be like a good hotel—open the year around.

WILLIAM LYON PHELPS[1]

Sometimes it is fun to create new ways of doing things. This principle certainly applies to the mental programming of goals and may increase interest and enthusiasm, thereby maintaining effectiveness despite the use of secondary programming techniques.

This chapter offers you a look at options and variations you can use to program your mind. We believe they will make mental programming more interesting, more fun, and may add to the overall effectiveness of your efforts.

If you ever happen to wander into a team training camp, you may find the athletes moving their lips, muttering, and/or making strange sounds. If you listen closely, you may hear them rhythmically chanting, repeating, or singing their affirmations. Often these chanted affirmations are done right along with their physical training. The advantages of this are that it can take the boredom out of training, make the time go faster, and allow for extra programming.

Singing, chanting, or grunting affirmations should not take the place of regular systematic mental programming sessions, but it can be a good supplemental method of reinforcing goals of all kinds.

There are indeed other mental programming models, which we will outline in this chapter. As you review the basic principles of mental programming theory, you may well be able to invent other programming systems more suitable to your individual requirements.

Some athletes have used these methods to reinforce goals during actual playing conditions. We know one tennis player who verbalizes—under his breath—affirmations that keep him from successive mistakes. If he mishits a serve to his backhand, he can be heard saying,

[1] Herbert V. Prochnow & Herbert V. Prochnow, Jr., *The Public Speaker's Treasure Chest* (New York: Harper & Row Publishers, Inc., 1964).

> I always hit great returns,
> I power them with ease,
> Serve it there again,
> Please, please, please.

The important thing to keep in mind is that no matter what system you use, the object is to place your well-defined goal into the subconscious mind in order for it to effectively help you bring that goal to fulfillment.

The goal may be to develop new belief systems about your capabilities; it may relate to enhancing mental or physical skills; or it could be directed toward desired achievements. It can be anything within natural law. Your goal is to put into thought form that which is verbal and visual.

CLOSET PROGRAMMING

There are several creative ways of repeating affirmations in addition to the usual way suggested for beginners in earlier chapters. More than one person has confided that he or she uses what we call "closet methods." They include taking affirmations and making silly simple rhyming ditties to repeat over and over while running or working out. Some people sing them in the shower or wildly in their cars as they drive along the freeway. Some "play" with them by using dialects and accents. These are all silly modes, which would totally embarrass the user in front of others. Thus the term "closet programming."

However, they do break the monotony of straight repetitions of affirmation droned on and on each session. And the subconscious seems to respond well to the variety of presentations, especially when the methods use heavy, dramatic emoting. Remember, emotion is a powerful force in programming and activating the subconscious to work on our goals.

WRITING AFFIRMATIONS

Many people report that writing affirmations is very helpful in programming goals. In its own way, it has the effect of causing the writer to reflect and imagine the goal more completely. It seems to have greater impressing potential for certain individuals.

Another version of writing affirmations is the mobile. For many years Jim Bennett has had reunions with groups that had taken his three-day seminars on this subject. These reunions are usually held in the home of one of the gracious alumni. It is not at all unusual to discover, upon occupying the bathroom, that the basic self-esteem and self-image affirmations are printed on cards that are made into mobiles and hung from the ceiling, to be read and repeated while doing other things. Some even have their most frequently used affirmations printed and plasticized, and then affix them to their shower walls.

There is no end to the creative variations that people come up with to be sure that their affirmations are always before them.

LAZY LEARNING: RECORDINGS

Other interesting and highly effective methods of programming goals in the subconscious mind are by means of recordings. Generally, any recording device will do, but specifically we refer to the recording of affirmations on audio cassette tapes. This method, a far cry from "on the hoof" systems, is a most convenient and effective approach once the initial recording has been made. And what lazier way can you think of than to sit passively in a chair while your tape recorder does all your programming for you?

The content of the affirmation tapes usually consists of the relaxation induction portion followed by a review of affirmations. It is easy to include time spaces and cues for using imagery in connection with each affirmation.

If you wish to, you or a friend can easily produce your own affirmation tape. Begin it by choosing one of the relaxation exercises in this book as a script that can be read, slowly, softly, and generally in a monotone style. When the induction is complete, just add, "Listen now to each of your affirmations, and as they are spoken, visualize each one as completely as you can."

Then record each affirmation on your tape. You may take each one in order and simply repeat it five times. For example,

"You always play aggressively and with enthusiasm."
"You always play aggressively and with enthusiasm."
"You always play aggressively and with enthusiasm."
"You always play aggressively and with enthusiasm."
"You always play aggressively and with enthusiasm."

If you wish to be more creative, present your affirmation with variations, changing the words around each time, perhaps using narrative form.

"You enjoy playing aggressively and with enthusiasm."
"You, Joe Athlete, are a very enthusiastic player and you do everything with enthusiasm."
"Your game is very aggressive and you find much pleasure in playing aggressively."
"Every day you are becoming more aggressive and enthusiastic in your play."

Notice that the tape recorder is talking to you, just as someone else might do, so you use the word "you" rather than "I."

Continue with this procedure by recording each affirmation that you are working with. Be sure to allow time for some imagery for each one. Thus, after the tape says, "Every day you are becoming more aggressive and enthusiastic in your play," take a minute and imagine yourself playing with enthusiasm. See yourself approaching the game in your special aggressive way and leave thirty to sixty seconds for this imagery.

When the programming portion is complete, you may record your termination of the session by reading one of the endings from the relaxation scripts in earlier chapters.

Many people have found that affirmation tapes work exceptionally well if listened to via a headset (earphones), and we recommend that you follow that procedure if possible. The programming impact is exciting for many, and the headset also helps to eliminate distractions.

LAZY LEARNING: SLUMBER TAPES

Perhaps one of the most ingenious and innovative programming systems is the "slumber tape." This is an affirmation tape played while you sleep. You need no more equipment than a tape recorder working from house power, a pillow speaker, and an endless loop cassette tape. One of twelve-minute duration will be suitable.

The tape, loaded with your affirmations, is turned on at bedtime and plays throughout the night while you sleep.

To prepare a slumber tape requires some care and precision. Although a relaxation induction is not used, it is important to write out your affirmations exactly as you want them said. Because you are using a loop tape, it is essential to time your presentation so that the ending does not overlap the beginning and thus erase it; and that the ending not come too soon, thus leaving a gap of silence, which we have found sometimes causes one to awaken from sleep.

Your script for the slumber tape should include some positive statements regarding "enjoying continuous, fulfilling rest and sleep which will leave you feeling completely rested, enthusiastic, full of positive spirits, and ready to charge into the day upon awaking in the morning."

HOW TO USE A SLUMBER TAPE

Place the cassette in your tape recorder and plug the pillow speaker into the monitor jack of the recorder. The tape recorder should be placed next to your bed so that the volume will be low. If you lie on your back, the speaker should be placed midway under the pillow. If you lie on your side, place the speaker so that it is in the approximate vicinity of your ear. Lay your head on the pillow and listen to the speaker and adjust the volume so that it is *just barely loud enough to hear clearly.* Do not set the volume too loud, or it can have a disturbing effect on your sleep. Do not have it too soft, or you will be unable to hear it. During the night you may roll over and away from the tape. Experience has shown that people do roll over and back and forth sufficiently to get the benefit from it anyway. The material on the tape plays through every twelve minutes, or five times an hour, throughout the night.

As you learned earlier, we are creating a condition (hypnosis) in which thought can be presented to the subconscious mind. We have learned that sleep is one of the times when thought can be effectively introduced to the subconscious mind on a repetitive basis. And so the slumber tape will provide you with continuous programming input into your subconscious mind while you sleep. We recommend that you use the tape every night for a week to see how it works for you.

If at times, however, you should find that the tape arouses or disturbs you, *do not struggle with the equipment,* but simply reach over and turn the tape off. *Make a strong mental note of that point.* You can always play the tape again another night. If in any way the tape is occasionally disturbing to your rest, feel free to shut it off rather than have it cause a negative response on your part. Sometimes it helps to use the tape only every other night or only occasionally. Some people are light sleepers and find that it keeps them awake. Others find that the sleep suggestions help them to sleep better. Each person is individual, so experiment with it and find which way works the best for you.

Remember that it is not intended that you pay attention to that tape. While you are sleeping your subconscious will hear the words whether you are at the conscious level or not. The subconscious hears thoughts anytime of the day. Remember, this slumber tape is designed to help reinforce your chosen goals in your mind. It is designed to help you become the fulfillment of your dreams. Use it as often as you can. If for any reason you find that the use of a slumber tape is unsatisfactory, feel free not to use it during sleep. Instead, experiment by listening to it, in a relaxed state, several times during the day.

Most of our discussion thus far has been about optional, creative, novel ways to program your goals with affirmations. Now let's look at innovative ways to program the subconscious with imagery as well. This is especially important material, not only for the variables that it offers but because it provides a real answer to those individuals who find it difficult to actually visualize.

PICTURES ON THE WALL

The first time we came across the use of pictures on the wall in lieu of visualizing was when Jim Bennett visited the home of a woman friend who weighed some 175 pounds. Her goal was to lose fifty pounds before taking a trip to Hawaii. She obtained a travel poster with the word "Hawaii" prominently printed across the top. The picture included rolling surf, palm trees, blue skies, and, of course, a gorgeous bikini-clad bathing beauty. Bennett's friend pasted a picture of her own face over the face of the lady on the poster.

Every day, when dressing, she took a good look at this picture while she affirmed her new weight and silhouette goals. This was truly creative mental programming. Can you think of some way that you could translate your goal into a visual picture like this? Perhaps one that shows you receiving a trophy for outstanding performance or one that depicts perfect form and technique in your sport. If you let your imagination run with this, you could come up with all kinds of goal-programming pictures!

MOVIES AND VIDEO

The use of visuals depicting ideal form, technique, and movement is proving to be an extremely effective mode of programming the athletic mind. To see, and record in the mind, perfect execution of a play or technique is a programming method that is gaining increasing acceptance among coaches.

It is not uncommon, for instance, for ski instructors to initiate training for beginners in the classroom rather than the slopes. Would-be skiers view, on screen, the various skiing maneuvers. These pictures are impressed in the subconscious minds of these viewers so well that when actual snow training commences, the actual muscle learning is accomplished much faster.

We found this to be true in our own experience with developmental training of athletes.

Bruce Magnuson, Olympic cyclist, was developing a four-man bicycle racing team. At one point in our mental training of this group, Bruce decided it would be helpful to show some films and slides of various champion riders. We agreed this would be useful and decided, in addition, that to really impress the subconscious minds of these men we would experiment with placing each of them in a hypnotic trance and let them look at the pictures in that state. The experiment appeared to be highly successful, and our subjective impression was that Bruce's team advanced in the mastery of their technique much faster than usually expected.

113

It is not necessary to be in a trance to gain the advantage of soaking up ideal models through viewing films and videotape. When a trance is lacking, we feel repetition can take over. If you wish to experiment on your own in the use of viewing films, try having your equipment all set to present and then just before turning it on, put yourself into a deep state of mental relaxation as per the exercises offered in earlier chapters. Once relaxed, open your eyes, turn your equipment on, and watch your films or slides.

In considering optional, creative mental programming techniques, the important thing to remember is that essentially the subconscious is not particular how the message is presented or by what source. *The main concern is that the message is presented and received, and that it is an accurate, literal presentation of a well-defined goal.*

Once you have mastered the basic mental programming techniques presented in this book (use them for eight weeks), feel free to experiment with these optional approaches, or if you wish, create some original methods that will work for you.

Remember, however, these creative methods are to be considered as supplemental approaches and not as substitutions for the basic techniques.

12 Time Management

Dost thou love life? Then do not squander time, for that is the
stuff life is made of.

BENJAMIN FRANKLIN[1]

Here you are—on the threshold of success! You have learned the steps necessary to vastly improve your sports performance; you are now ready to become a far better athlete than you may have thought possible.

Don't stop now. Don't look at this book as only an interesting reading
experience. Use it as it was meant to be used—as a guide along the road to
your athletic dreams. Those dreams can become your reality.

It takes so little time to become better. Just imagine the surprise of
your friends as they see significant improvements in your ability. They will
suspect that you have been taking lessons on the sly. They will ask you where
and from whom, but you will be able honestly to deny that you have been
spending money and time on secret sessions with some master or mistress of
your sport.

This is no exaggeration. It happens all the time. People do notice the
difference. You will not be alone in the appreciation of your new level of
skill, and your *real* friends will be as delighted as you about the change.

However, there will be those who do not understand; and those who do
not believe in the power of the mind. Still, even they will have to admit to
your success, and some filtering on your part will keep their attitudes from
diluting your enjoyment.

Surprisingly, it is often those same doubters who would spend hours at
physical practice but no time at mental practice, perhaps simply because they
don't understand how the mind can be used for this purpose. But you do
know, so do it now so that you can enjoy the ample benefits that are available to you.

---

[1] Herbert V. Prochnow & Herbert V. Prochnow, Jr., *The Public Speaker's Treasure
Chest* (New York: Harper & Row Publishers, Inc., 1964).

Whatever you do, don't hesitate because you think you may not have the time for the mental programming exercises. Read the rest of this chapter first, for it will help you to find all the time you need. And more often than not, you will find more than you need!

FINDING TIME

Time can be a friend—or one of your worst enemies. When you have all the time you want to finish a task or enjoy a vacation, you tend to think of time as an ally. But if you are taking a final exam in a tough college course, or are standing blindfolded before a firing squad, you would likely look at time as a fleeting friend indeed.

Time is an exhaustible resource for each individual; our lives have a finite limit, just as a day has a finite limit of twenty-four hours. Nevertheless, far too many people look at time as being open-ended. There will always be more time tomorrow. Projects, ideas, dreams, and even daily tasks are put off—often to be forever unrealized—because people do not perceive the erosion of their fixed allotment of time. And what is worse, many people don't care.

What person has not said, "Boy, I'd like to do that, but I just don't have the time"?

Do you really believe that person? We find it hard to do so simply because the average person is a very poor manager of time. The individual making that statement could almost always find the necessary time by learning to budget that commodity. Or if he was the rare soul who was really that time-limited, he would replace some other existing activity with the one he'd "like to do." And that is actually a priority problem.

Have you ever been a member of a volunteer organization where all the members had assignment to report on for the monthly meeting, but half of them arrived unprepared because, "I just ran out of time." However, when you check the prior evening's TV schedule, you discover that there was a block-buster program on the tube. What these people did was to establish priorities for their time.

Remember these two words in relation to time: *budget* and *priority*. We will discuss them more later.

We all know countless people (often ourselves) who profess an interest in something but back away from it because "I just don't have the time." This type of reaction is usually an attempt to be sociable. A friend enjoys a certain activity, so we try to establish rapport by pretending a desire to do the same thing, even though we aren't really that interested. But the good old "I don't have time" excuse allows us to be friendly without making a commitment to involvement.

Some people go a step further and use that excuse to avoid work and still enjoy reflected glory. Take, for example, some members of direct selling organizations and would-be writers. At annual conventions there are dozens of people who get a chance to enjoy all the hoopla, banquets, and panels and yet never accomplish anything in their chosen area of interest. When asked what they are currently doing, they say, "Oh, I've got something really good on the back burner, *and as soon as I find the time,* I'll be able to finish it."

After the convention, these people return home and tell their friends, "Oh, yes, I attended the Famous Organization Convention last week and had a chance to chat with Mr. Famous Person."

From this, their friends will infer that the conventioneer is deserving of status as a real practicing super salesman or author.

The sad part is that many of those people have the talent to be the successful person they dream of being. A few of them are only kidding themselves and are hangers-on, but most truly wish to apply themselves and need only to learn time management. It is this majority group that we can help in this chapter.

Because you are reading this book, we assume you are interested in improving some aspect of your sports activity. We don't want you to fail in that ambition because you may feel that you don't have time to do the mental programming. We are convinced that virtually everyone has the time somewhere, and this chapter is designed to help you find it.

Better yet, time management—like the principles of Mental Dynamics—is not restricted to sports alone. It can be applied to your whole life, and allow you to be in charge, to control your time and avoid the frustration and stress that come from indecision and nonproductive time.

We assume that you have read and understood the previous chapters and are therefore fully aware of the exciting potential that awaits you. So now we are going to show you how to integrate the mental programming process into your daily life; and, for most of you, how to do so without taking any time away from your other required tasks. In fact, if you gain a full understanding of time management, you may have more productive time than you used to—even after scheduling programming sessions.

First of all, you must have *desire*, for it is the prime mover. With it you will have the resolve to use Mental Dynamics and to find the time to do so. After reading this chapter you will learn that time can be a positive force in your life, a force that feeds desire and opens the door to improved sports performance.

Desire comes in many levels of intensity. It can be enhanced by mental programming, just as we showed you earlier how to use Mental Dynamics to improve your attitude about dull physical practice routines—or anything else, for that matter.

THE FOUR STEPS
TO SUCCESSFUL TIME MANAGEMENT

With desire, and some basic time management concepts from this chapter, you will be in control of your life and will see how easy it will be to find the time for your Mental Dynamics sessions—the sessions that can lead you to boundless opportunities in sports. So read the following steps with care. They are your path to being a successful time manager.

STEP 1: TAKE AN HONEST, OBECTIVE SURVEY OF JUST HOW YOU SPEND YOUR TIME. Don't confuse this with a time budget, which comes later. For now, you must simply record the use of your time, without any changes in your daily routine. You need to know exactly how you are spending every minute in order to get the information you need for the next step. You don't need any fancy materials for this step, just a small notebook and a pencil or pen. The notebook should be small enough to fit in your pocket or purse because it must be kept up to date on a regular—almost hourly—basis. It's too easy to forget small details as the day wears on, so the entries have to be made frequently. Several small increments of time can add up to a significant number, and therefore need to be accounted for. Any type of effort less than that will result in time *estimates* instead of the hard data you will need for the next step.

Let's go back to our friend Jenny Athlete, whom we met in Chapter 5. She took advantage of these time management principles to find time for her programming sessions, and ultimately to design a time budget which allowed her to expand into other areas as well.

Jenny kept her notebook for a week, since most people operate on a weekly cycle as a minimum. The longer the period over which you record the data, the better the results. But for most people, a week will be plenty.

Here are the opening entries that Jenny made on her first day:

Time Period	Activity	Elapsed Time (minutes)
6:30-6:40	Alarm went off. Spent time in bed before getting up.	10
6:40-6:50	Took shower.	10
6:50-7:20	Dried hair, brushed teeth, put on makeup, and dressed.	30
7:20-7:35	Read paper and drank coffee, which Joe had prepared.	15
7:35-7:50	Made breakfast.	15
7:50-8:01	Started to eat breakfast.	11

Time Period	Activity	Elapsed Time (minutes)
8:01-8:23	Phone call from friend.	22
8:23-8:36	Finished eating breakfast.	13
8:36-8:57	Washed dishes and cleaned kitchen.	21
	Subtotal	147

This may seem like a lot of work at first glance, but it isn't really that demanding. It even gets to be fun after you establish the habit of making regular entries. In a short while you will become very conscious of how you spend your time, but it is vitally important that you do not alter your normal routine. Your ability to become a good time manager requires good starting data, which truly reflect your current life-style. Try to avoid subtle—sometimes unconscious—changes in your habits as you become aware of increments of wasted time.

It won't take more than two or three days to notice some of your bigger contributions to time inefficiency. Even better, you will be pleased and amazed to have this unique view of your life—a viewpoint that most people never see. With this information you will be able to define the problem of time mismanagement, a problem many people don't realize they have. Clearly, as in any area of life, there can be no solution to a problem until you can get a firm grip on—or definition of—the problem itself.

Now then, let's look back to the first page of Jenny's journal. She has made one mistake which she later corrected. Did you pick it up? . . . . She should have started her record at midnight rather than her wake-up time. It makes it easier to work with the data later if each day has a common starting point, and the chances are that she won't get up at the same time every morning, especially on weekends. That means her first entry each day should be a sleep period, and on most days her final entry will also be a sleep period that ends at midnight.

Record your elapsed times in minutes and make a subtotal at the bottom of each page. When the day is done, you should have a grand total of 1,440 minutes.

Working with minutes rather than with combinations of minutes and hours will make it easier to manipulate the data later and will avoid mistakes when switching back and forth between the two units of time.

STEP 2: Now that you have a full day's data, you can *start categorizing and arranging it in a fashion that is more meaningful to you.* You will want to combine all the common time increments into a single entry. For example, if you had seven phone conversations during the day, you should combine them to find out how much time you spent on the phone.

When you are through, you will have a list that looks like the following list, which Jenny made up from her first day.

Activity	Time (minutes)
Sleep	450
Work (part-time job)	225
Work break	15
Work transportation	30
Eating time (three meals)	100
Telephone calls	58
Cooking meals	15
Washing dishes	21
Other household chores	27
Watching TV	90
Tennis match	90
Miscellaneous transportation	24
Shopping	102
Personal visiting	97
Personal hygiene	51
Reading	45
Subtotal	1,440

Now you can see a picture forming of Jenny's life and how she spends her time.

Some people will prefer to arrange the items in descending order of amount of time spent on each activity. In other words, for Jenny, the third item would have been shopping, the fourth would have been eating time, and so on down to the smallest time-consuming item.

You will notice that the total number of minutes must still add up to 1,440.

You will also have to make commonsense judgments about categorizing some items. If you make a phone call about business, it is actually work time, but if you make a personal call (at work or not), it should be listed under "telephone calls." Remember, you're accounting for your actual time use, not the time your employer is paying you for. The important thing to remember is that the data must be meaningful to you, so categorize it and arrange it to give you the most insight into your personal use of time.

Here are some of the more common areas of wasted time:

Bed. Especially if you have no early morning demands. It's very easy to roll over and grab an extra half hour whether you need it or not.

TV. You can always cut here.

Telephone. Most people can easily cut this category without loss of friendship or effective communication.

Eating. A light meal at home will generally take less time than eating out.

Coffee Breaks/Reading.

Miscellaneous or Undefined. This is an interesting, and often surprising, category. As you log data into your notebook, you may discover that you cannot remember exactly how you spent all your time. This lapse will occur most often when you forget to make frequent entries. Lump all these time periods into this category. When you summarize your data at day's end, you may be surprised at the size of this item. If it is more than thirty minutes, you should make more frequent entries in your notebook.

STEP 3: *Prioritize your time.* Even though you have identified areas of waste, you may find it difficult to change old habits. Thus, you must decide which activities are most important, and list them—in writing—in their order of importance. Then go down the list and decide how much time, if any, you are willing to give up in favor of some other activity. When you are done, you will have a good idea of the amount of the "slop" you have to work with.

You don't have to eliminate whole categories if you don't want to; rather, take a couple of minutes away from several different categories if that is easier for you. Either way, it will become very apparent that twenty to thirty minutes of spare time can be found. In most cases a great deal more can be found, because you have used your data and your priorities to determine what is really important in your life.

Stop a moment and think about what this is doing for you. Perhaps for the first time in your life you are in control of your time, determining how *you* want to use it and how much time *you* want to allocate to each activity.

This means that you are also in control of your sports destiny, because you will have plenty of time to use the Mental Dynamics exercises you learned earlier.

STEP 4: *Make a time budget—in writing—so that you will always be aware of your time allocations.* Writing down your time budget will serve the same purpose as writing down your sports goals and plans of action, as we suggested earlier. It will help to visually implant the whole idea into your subconscious.

Here's a sample of Jenny's time budget for the early part of one day. You may want to compare it with the entries she made in her notebook before she arranged and budgeted her time.

Time Period	Activity	Elapsed Time (minutes)
Midnight-6:20	Sleep.	380
6:20-6:40	Mental Dynamics.	20
6:40-6:55	Physical exercises.	15

Time Period	Activity	Elapsed Time (minutes)
6:55-7:05	Took shower.	10
7:05-7:30	Dried hair, brushed teeth, applied makeup, and dressed.	25
7:30-7:50	Read paper and drank coffee.	20
7:50-8:20	Ate breakfast.	30
8:20-8:45	Washed dishes and cleaned kitchen.	25
	Subtotal	525

You can see that Jenny made some significant improvements in her time usage. She made time not only for her Mental Dynamics exercises but for some physical exercises as well.

Jenny set the following priorities on her time:

1. She got up ten minutes earlier and didn't dawdle in bed.
2. She made more efficient use of reading and grooming time.
3. She asked her friends not to call before 9:00 A.M. so she could spend uninterrupted time with Joe at breakfast.

It becomes quite obvious that Jenny has achieved far greater control over her life with virtually no sacrifices. What exciting vistas are now open to her! She has already expanded her mental and physical opportunities; not only for sports but for life in general; not only for fun but for health and well-being. And according to her time budget, it is not yet 9:00 A.M.! Just think what she can achieve with a full day at her command.

LEARNING HOW TO BE A TIME MANAGER

You now know how to manage time. But is this enough? Probably not. Knowing how to do something is no guarantee that the individual has the resolve to apply the new knowledge, especially over the long haul. Too often we see people who start out with great enthusiasm to lose weight, stop smoking, get rich, or become better athletes only to fade out and slip back into old habits.

The program we have just outlined can be very effective, but to become a true time manager for the rest of your life, you should apply the principles of Mental Dynamics. It is important not only to know how to do the things necessary to become a time manager; it is also vital to become a time manager through application of your knowledge and *by creating a self-image of that kind of person.*

You must go beyond learning *how to*; you must learn *how to be*!

A possessor of how-to knowledge may do the things he has learned how to do with varying degrees of success, depending on the extent of his previous practice. But if he has not become that kind of person it will generally be done haltingly and inconsistently. When you become a particular kind of person, you do things automatically, smoothly, and skillfully. As an example, in sports and recreation, many of you know how to bowl, how to fish, how to play tennis or golf. But you did not necessarily become involved sufficiently that you became a bowler, a fisherman, tennis player, or golfer. Some have learned how to play the piano and yet have never become a pianist. Likewise, knowing how to type does not make you a typist. Some of you may know how to sell but have not become salespersons. Many of us know how to make decisions, but because we never became a decision maker we may not make decisions with regularity and consistency. Most of us know about delegating responsibility, yet if we never become a delegator, we may find some problems in passing on responsibilities appropriately. You may know about setting goals and you may know how to set goals, but that does not guarantee that you will be a goal setter. (Refer back to Chapter 5 for a refresher on goals.) You may have learned how to organize your work, your time, your day, and yet if you never become an organizer, you will find that things still get piled up. Life is still a confused mess. And finally, you may have learned how to manage time, but if you have never become a time manager, then you're still a step away from success.

Part of being or becoming anything implies that self-image factors must be considered. Self-image psychology says, "The way one sees oneself is essentially how one will consistently perform." Understanding self-image psychology further, we can see that it is possible to choose, define, and design self-image traits. Plant them in the mind and eventually become what we choose. In other words, you can indeed design a self-image as an effective time manager and then define this self-image carefully. Finally, you can introduce it to the subconscious mind in such a way that you will subsequently grow into that kind of person.

Does this sound too good to be true? Almost like magic? Yes, it is almost like magic, but it is a magic you can make work by using the programming techniques we have already described in Chapter 6.

You can program your subconscious to create an effective self-image of a time manager. To help you think that way about time in relation to yourself, consider what might be your beliefs and philosophy of time, for how you relate to time, how you use it, will indeed be influenced by your belief systems concerning it.

Here are a few reflections on time that illustrate our point.

Time is all things to all people.
If only I had more time.
Time on my hands.
Time flies.
Time drags.
Time is different things to different people. To an Arabian herdsman time is for musing. For a busy physician time is for getting behind (or maybe ahead).
Had a great time.
Had a lousy time.
Had the time of my life.
There isn't any time left.
Time is urgent.
Just in the knick of time.
Not this time.
Time to get home.
Now is the time.
Time is for recording: time of birth, time of death, time of arrival or departure, time of engagement, wedding time.
How quickly it went.
How long it took.
Time is a scapegoat. I would have done it if I'd had more time.
Time ran out on us.
It's that time of the month.
Time runs things for us.
Time out, time in, time's up. Time to go home. Time to work. Time to rest, time for a smoke, time to go to bed.

Time. What is it? Some have too much, some not enough. But somehow we all have it and we have not yet learned how the haves could possibly share with the have-nots. See what we have done with time. We blame everything on it. Sometimes we give it credit. You can't see it, touch it, taste it, or hear it. But time is not an enemy, nor is it the cause of tension or pressure. Time should be considered our friend. You see, time is really what we make it. It offers us a second chance. If we look, we'll see that it allows us to make good things happen. It allows us to be productive. It permits us to earn. It opens the door to love and to raise families if we will but use it for that. It allows us to relax and to recreate. Time is really neutral and amoral. It's passive. It is simply here for us to express ourselves in work, career, family, community, recreation, art, religion, anything we choose. We can use time to achieve our potential. Or we can botch things up. But don't blame it on time. Time is permissive. It allows us to be, to do, to think, to create, and to succeed. The attitude that we hold about time can let us grow. Without time there would be no life. Perhaps time is a gift, but a gift equally apportioned among every living being. We do not use time. We exist within it. We function within it and that is what time management is all about: how to function effectively in time.

If you have been guilty of thinking of yourself as a scatterbrain or as an unorganized person, then use Mental Dynamics to change your self-image—right now, today! Chapters 5 through 7 have already told you how.

Combine this new self-image with the four steps you learned in the first half of this chapter, and you will never be a slave to time again.

You will have built a friendship with time and will no longer have to use time as a scapegoat. Time will be a giver of opportunity, a partner in the playground of life.

Use it, and control it, to live your life to its fullest. And just incidentally, use it to become a better athlete than ever before.

In summary, here are the key items to remember about time management.

1. Take a survey of your use of time—a written record.
2. Arrange and summarize the data so that it is meaningful to you.
3. Make a written priority list so you will know which activities in your life are really important to *you.*
4. Make a time budget based on your recorded data and your priority list.
5. Use Mental Dynamics to create a self-image of a time manager so that what you have learned will become a permanent part of your life.

13 Creative Thinking and Problem Solving in Sports

> Eighty percent of the time, there is a way out of trouble. You just have to know how to look for it.
>
> ARNOLD PALMER[1]

The 1981 American League baseball season was still in the first half of its schedule, but the Seattle Mariners had already posted a dismal record of 6 wins and 18 losses. Nothing was going right. Team morale was "in the pits." Individually, and as a team, a lot of talent and potential was going to waste.

Rene Lachemann, manager of the Mariners' Spokane farm team, was called in to take over the reins as manager of the parent club on May 5. His problem: how to turn this club around!

Here was a situation requiring the very best creativity and problem solving ability that Rene Lachemann could muster. In a relatively short time—one week into the 1981 "second season"—Lachemann was able to lead his club to a very respectable .500 winning percentage posted since his arrival. And the club reached the new plateau with a flourish—a shutout performance on August 15 over the Minnesota Twins, which also left the team in first place in the American League West.

With virtually the same players and environment as his predecessor, Lachemann clearly solved a sports problem. And though personality and experience were factors, there is no doubt that Lachemann introduced imagination and creativity into the formula that turned his club around.

This type of ability is natural for some people, but the good news is that this ability can also be learned and enhanced by people who are not born with this talent.

For years problem solving techniques and creative thinking systems have been taught, studied, and applied by people and organizations from nearly all walks of life—but rarely if ever do we hear of any formal or scientific approach to solving problems in sports. Businesses do so all the time. In

---

[1] Frank Litsky, *Superstars* (Secaucus, N.J.: Derbibooks, Inc., 1975).

fact, it has been said, "The business of business is problem solving." Many companies encourage their executives to take time away from their offices to *clear their heads* so they can work on creative problem solving. This is an enlightened management technique based on the well-understood knowledge that many creative solutions arise full born from the subconscious mind rather than from the turmoil of the frequently troubled conscious mind. The conscious mind is used to help input all the problem parameters to the sub-conscious mind, and then the conscious mind must be relaxed and removed from the problem, preferably in a tension-free environment, so that the sub-conscious mind is left alone to work the problem, largely shielded from the disruptive forces of other emotional inputs.

Increasingly more companies are allowing their executives and middle managers to take longer lunch hours if they use the time to do something physical such as running, swimming, or tennis. This not only improves their physical health but also allows their subconscious to create solutions to work problems. It is this same force at night that brings forth so much construc-tive thinking, hunches, and abrupt ideas while we rest or sleep. Maxwell Maltz[2] summarizes this concept when he says, ". . . creative ideas are not consciously thought out by forebrain thinking, but come automatically, spontaneously, and somewhat like a bolt out of the blue, when the conscious mind has let go of the problem and is engaged in thinking of something else."

As another example, it's not uncommon to hear of professionals and businesspeople "working" on the golf course by getting away from the prob-lem and relaxing. For many, this is the best way to come up with many important answers and solutions.

John Williams, in his book *The Knack of Using Your Subconscious Mind*, tells of a businessman who combines golf and business. In a letter he says,

> I've learned how to make a golf game pay for the time it takes. Instead of letting myself work up to the hour when I'm to leave for the links without any thought of what I want the afternoon's relaxation to do for me, I make it a point, before leaving my office, to dig into some problem just far enough to get the elements lined up clearly in my mind or on paper. Then I put them out of my conscious thought— shove them back into the subconscious—and forget them while I play golf. As a matter of fact, one simply can't think consciously about business problems out on the links. (I know because I've tried.) The problem simmers away. Sometimes it's all cooked into a solution by the time I'm back in my street clothes; sometimes it isn't. But I've noticed that following an afternoon of golf, the solution is nearly always ready by the time I reach my desk the next morning, and I

[2]Maxwell Maltz, *Psycho-Cybernetics* (Englewood Cliffs, N.J.: Prentice-Hall, Inc., 1960).

know my afternoon wasn't wasted. Since I've learned this "fireless cooking" technique, I always think of my country club as my 18 hole office. The trick is on focusing on the problem for ½ hour or so before you leave the office, and cutting it up into small pieces for easier "cooking."[3]

A French scientist, named Fehr, commented once that most of his good ideas came to him when he was not directly working on a problem and that most of the discoveries made by his peers happened when they were away from their work.[4]

CREATIVE PROBLEM SOLVING IN SPORTS

Creative problem solving, especially that which is done at the subconscious level, is something truly needed in sports, just as much as in other walks of life.

Actually, creative thinking and problem solving is a process used to some degree by everyone, including coaches and athletes. But it is often not used knowingly or as a regular, systematic, scientific procedure. It tends to just happen—for instance, when you see someone you know pass by. You know the individual well, yet for some reason his name will not come to you. It's on the tip of your tongue, but the harder you try, the more elusive it is. Finally, you tell yourself, "Oh, well, it will come to me later." And sure enough, later on, when you have taken your conscious mind off the problem, the subconscious computer spontaneously gives you an automatic readout. "George Smith—of course!"

Another example of the subconscious working on a problem spontaneously and without using any conscious method is when you plan to rise at 4:00 A.M. to go fishing or to catch an early plane. More often than not, even though your clock is set for 4:00 A.M.—and you normally don't rise until 6:30—your subconscious alarm system has you waking up at exactly 3:59. The subconscious is always awake and always ready to help out.

Creative problem solving is a method that can be used with dramatic effect in sport. Four areas where it can be successfully applied are:

1. Game strategy
2. Equipment improvement

[3]John K. Williams, *The Knack of Using Your Subconscious Mind* (Englewood Cliffs, N.J.: Prentice-Hall, Inc., 1952).

[4]Maxwell Maltz, *Psycho-Cybernetics* (Englewood Cliffs, N.J.: Prentice-Hall, Inc., 1960).

3. Technique diagnosis and correction
4. Blocks to success

GAME STRATEGY. Jack Patera, head coach of the Seattle Seahawks National Football League club, has established a reputation for exciting, non-traditional gamesmanship. More than once he has astounded opposing teams with unconventional and highly creative plays. We don't know how much Jack Patera's creativity comes from his conscious mind versus his subconscious mind, but the point is: that is exactly the kind of product the subconscious is capable of delivering. When the conscious effort runs out of steam—for whatever reason—the subconscious can deliver the goods if you will let it do so.

One of Patera's most creative games was shown on ABC Monday Night Football the evening of October 29, 1979, at Atlanta. The exciting game-turning plays were based on game films and Patera's willingness to test the limits of conventional practice.

In the second quarter the Falcons were ahead 14-0. Seattle had the ball on Atlanta's 34-yard line, fourth down and 5 yards to go for a first down. The Seahawks lined up for a field goal try, with first-string quarterback Jim Zorn prepared to take the snap and hold the ball for the kicker as he had countless times before. Only this time Zorn took the snap and ran for a touchdown.

National Football League quarterbacks may occasionally pass from field goal formation, but they simply do not *run* from that formation. But Zorn did—by plan—and the Seahawks were back in the game.

Later in the game, Seattle was on the Atlanta 37-yard line, once again with a fourth down and 5 yards to go. Zorn lined up again to take the snap and hold the ball for kicker Efren Herrera. Zorn took the pass and stood quickly upright. The defense momentarily froze, not knowing whether the left-handed quarterback was going to throw or run again. Meanwhile, the chunky Herrera sprinted around the right end unmolested, where he gobbled up Zorn's quick pass and ran to the 1-yard line before the defense recovered. Seattle went on to score another touchdown and eventually won the game to the delight of millions of TV viewers. Even Howard Cossell approved.

Incidentally, it was Efren Herrera who stated on a television interview that his kicking technique is 80 percent mental!

This kind of game strategy ingeniously planned and executed turned more than one game around for Patera and his Seahawks.

Doug Ruffin, high-ranking Northwest tennis pro, tells of using his subconscious mind to plot out innovative defensive moves on the tennis court. As he says, "If your game is going poorly, you have two options: play your game better or creatively change the game around."

Remember Amos Alonzo Stagg? For all his greatness as a football coach, Stagg was truly a great creative problem solver. He is credited with influencing football strategy in many ways. It was he who invented the man-in-motion, the shift, onside kick, the quick kick, and the field goal from placement as we now know it (before that it was the dropkick). And Patera can thank Stagg also for inventing the fake field goal.

EQUIPMENT. Amos Stagg did not limit his greatness to game strategy. For example, when he needed a more effective means of training his players to tackle better, he solved the problem by inventing the tackling dummy. Furthermore, baseball players can thank Stagg for his invention of the batting cage. In addition, he is also credited with developing the troughs that catch swimming pool overflow.

We don't know from his own records that Stagg used his subconscious in a regular systematic way to be so creative in sports. But there is little doubt that he did so in an informal manner, for all great thinkers give credit to hunches, inspiration, dreams of sudden insight, for their innovative thinking. Indeed, these are all manifestations of the subconscious at work.

There are countless examples of people who have used affirmations to activate their subconscious to focus on a specific problem. Incredible results have been obtained from patient application of this technique.

Nikola Tesla, a famous scientist, and Louis Agassiz, the distinguished American naturalist, both used their subconscious minds many times to make significant contributions to their fields of study. Dr. Frederick Banting developed the use of insulin for diabetics as a result of guidance from his subconscious mind while asleep.

These men probably used affirmations unknowingly by working on their problems so hard in a conscious state. Stagg likely did the same. When you see their results, you can begin to imagine the potential available to us all by using a more systematic approach for utilizing the power of the subconscious.

Sometimes creative thinking and problem solving may go too far or be too radical for acceptance by others. In tennis, for instance, the spaghetti string racquet appeared to give the user an unfair advantage over others, and consequently, it was banned.

The fiberglass vaulting pole is still another example of using the creative mind to bring about change and improvement in athletic equipment. With it, the average height of pole vaulting increased dramatically.

TECHNIQUE. Creative problem solving may best be used by an athlete in the area of solving problems related to game technique. The stroke is not quite right, the swing is off, the ball is hooking, the stance may be off.

Usually a player will spend hours by himself, and with others, analyzing or introspectingly puzzling over some problem, often with no concrete results. In fact, the athlete will use continuous ruminations such as, "What am I doing wrong?" When heard over and over again, the literal-minded subconscious often responds as if they were an affirmation: "I am doing something wrong. My stroke is wrong. My swing is off." And as you have already learned, an affirmation often repeated is received by the subconscious and translated into a reality.

If conscious-mind analysis of a slump or other technique problem does not produce results quickly, consider using creative problem solving with your subconscious mind instead.

In effect, you will be talking to your subconscious mind, as if it were another person or entity and simply state your need: "Subconscious (or Sub, or George, or Mary, or whatever you choose to call it), lately I've been having a problem with my batting. How about telling me what I need to know to make the correction needed to get back on track."

Following the steps that will be outlined at the end of this chapter, you will be amazed at how often you will actually "hear" from the subconscious with a suggestion or idea. It will usually be like an obvious insight: "Of course, why didn't I think of that before?"

Instead of telling you the solution (popping the idea into your conscious mind), the subconscious will sometimes simply go ahead and solve the problem for you. You will suddenly begin to perform your technique properly. Either way, it is a wonderful help.

Creative problem solving through your subconscious mind is a skill that you can develop. Of course, like all other skills, you become as good as you apply yourself to it. In this mode, however, applying yourself means practice and more practice by giving assignments to the subconscious mind and then letting go of the problem while your subconscious works with it.

Remember, the subconscious mind does not work with a problem while you or your conscious mind is working on it. As the famous Bob Gates, Jr., once said, "My art, as all art, flows from being, not thinking."

BLOCKS TO SUCCESS. Sometimes we know the blocks we must overcome to be successful, and at other times we do not. Blocks can also affect your sport indirectly, as in the case of Jackie Jensen, the former Boston Red Sox slugger, whose apparent dislike of flying caused an early termination of a sparkling career. This type of problem can frequently be improved or cured through mental programming.

Another well-known block is the infamous "writer's block." Those occur on days when the writer stares at a blank piece of paper—sometimes for hours—and nothing comes from the mind except the figurative "blood on the brow."

We know writers who solve that block by starting to type anything that comes to mind, whether it relates to the subject or not. Within a couple of pages the material starts to flow easily. A few days later, when the pump-primed material is proofed, the writer will typically find the first page or so to be garbage; but the subsequent pages are good, and—what's really exciting—some of the writing is far better than the writer thought he or she was capable of producing.

Can you see what caused that to happen? The subconscious had all the necessary information but had to be set free. The writer turned the subconscious loose by typing garbage and concentrating on that. Within minutes the subconscious responded with a smooth flow of prose to break the block.

This system can be used to discover hidden blocks or to find a solution to a known problem.

TAPPING THE CREATIVE POWER OF THE SUBCONSCIOUS

Okay, let's list the specific steps you can use for creative thinking and problem solving.

1. Try to define the problem. Diagnose it to the best of your ability. Write it down if that helps.
2. Gather as much data relating to the problem as you can. Talk with others. Again, write it down if you wish. List pro and con items.
3. Brainstorm the problem. At this point, it sometimes happens that a solution is found through these conscious efforts.
4. If no answer is forthcoming, then take some time to think about all the aspects of the problem. When you've "had it" mentally, and your conscious mind is beat, it's time to back away from the whole thing.
5. Go fishing, or whatever it takes to forget the problem completely.
6. Relax, and let the answer come to you at its own pace. Usually, the answer will come at, or before, the time it is needed.
7. The answer can come in many forms. Sometimes you will recognize it as a substantial increase in your confidence. Sometimes you will get a partial solution based on the data available. Very often it will be a complete solution which will frequently appear as a bolt out of the blue.
8. Be sure to write the answer down, especially if it comes to you in the night. Otherwise, it will slip away like a dream.

In summary, remember that the subconscious mind within each of us is indeed considered by many as the genius within. When this inner power is recognized, and tapped, it can immensely enhance one's capability to think creatively and solve problems.

In sport this power can be used in all areas. Specifically, we have looked at its use in game strategy, equipment improvement, technique enhancement, blocks to success, and the steps to use in tapping the power of the subconscious.

Finally, let us leave you with a suggestion that will ensure long-term, consistent success in your use of creative thinking and problem solving techniques. As you develop your positive self-image through the use of Mental Dynamics, be sure to incorporate the following affirmation into your subconscious programming sessions: "I AM A SUCCESSFUL CREATIVE THINKER AND PROBLEM SOLVER."

14 "Head" Coach

> Winning isn't worthwhile unless one has something finer and
> nobler behind it. When I reach the soul of one of my boys with
> an idea or ideal or a vision, then I have done my job as a coach.
>
> AMOS ALONZO STAGG[1]

Psychology in sport is not very new. In fact, it has been in use about as long as people have played in organized competitive sports. But sports psychology as a system or science has only recently come into its own. In the recent past many coaches were satisfied to use their own personal brand of psychology to motivate their players to peak performance. They used everything from high-pitch emotional pep talks to positive or negative reinforcement. Praise and threats. Rewards and intimidation. There were no limits to the variety of psychological ploys.

Today, coaches and players alike are becoming more sophisticated. In varying degrees they realize that all things begin in the mind of the individual. Before you raise yourself out of a chair, the thought must be in your mind. Likewise, they now understand that before you can raise your confidence level, that thought must also be in your mind. Before you break a school record, that possibility must also be in your mind.

So more and more, coaches are helping their players to recognize their potential to ever increase their skills and abilities.

In professional sport this is even more true. Increasingly, professional teams employ individuals of various backgrounds to assist their players mentally. Psychologists, psychiatrists, spiritual and religious leaders have all been used. In fact, the Tucson Sky (professional volleyball team of the IVA) had their own witch doctor who spent much of each game placing hexes on the visiting team.

Author Bennett served as Mental Dynamics consultant to the Seattle Smashers Professional Volleyball team. The players were sometimes unsure of what to call him or how to refer to him. One player introduced him to his

138   [1]Frank Litsky, *Superstars* (Secaucus, N.J.: Derbibooks, Inc., 1975).

friends as "the team shrink." Though that was hardly the correct term to use, it points out the relative newness of the specialty and the awkwardness of terminology.

One player solved the problem of titles by referring to Bennett as the "head" coach, And still another called him the Ann Landers of sport. Eventually, the two concepts came together and led to a question/answer column known as the "Head" Coach, designed for people in sports who wanted their mental problems solved. We present a few select columns here to give some specific examples of our concepts and to further your understanding of the principles of Mental Dynamics.

Example 1

QUESTION: I have used autosuggestion and other self-programming systems for years but can't seem to improve my fielding skills. I play the infield and tell myself, "I will not bobble any grounders," but my errors are increasing, not decreasing. Can you help me?

ANSWER: Your problem reminds me of an amusing demonstration of the mental process called the Law of Reversed Effect. To illustrate: Close your eyes and try very hard not to picture a polar bear sitting on a small block of ice! It's difficult to get that crazy bear out of your mind once you have created a mental image of him.

In the same fashion you are committing a more destructive error than bobbling the ball. It is one made by many people who practice mental programming without a true understanding of the principles. Mental programming is a fantastic tool when used correctly, but when it isn't, it can have a reverse effect. The error you are making is that of programming the *problem* instead of the *solution*.

Whenever using verbal self-suggestion, make every effort to state it in positive terms. State what you wish for, not what you fear or dread.

Remember, the verbal suggestions are received by your subconscious, which tends to create realities from them. Your verbal statements also trigger imagery, which is an even more potent subconscious programming force.

Thus, the statement "I will not bobble any grounders" is suggestive of the idea and imagery of bobbling. You are, in effect, mentally programming the errors. Others make the same mistake with such statements as, "I'll never fumble the ball." Or "I will not muff that spare."

Those suggestions are poison! They must be restated to fit the desired goals. In your case, say, "I enjoy fielding grounders perfectly." (See yourself doing it!)

Mental programming involves verbal statements and visual imagery. In the future, be sure that they both reflect what you want, not what you don't want.

Example 2

QUESTION: Every time I compete in "unfriendly" country, I get uptight when the fans ride me. Any suggestions?

ANSWER: Yours is one of the oldest problems faced by athletes. The home-town fans naturally root for the favorites, but sometimes they get carried away and are pretty rough on visitors. This is one of the main reasons road competition is considered to be a disadvantage to visitors. Other reasons include unfamiliar playing area, different climate and altitude, and traveling fatigue. I take it when you use the words "every time" that you really mean it. If so, I suggest that you make an attitude adjustment. Learn to think of host country as partisan, or simply loyal to the local talent, just as the fans in your hometown (hopefully) are loyal to you. Remember, spectators like to participate too, and, right or wrong, one way to do it is by cheering and jeering.

When you play well and sportsmanlike, the fans will respect you, win or lose, even if they do try to test you psychologically or help their own players along by giving you a bad time. Just listen to the fans when a visitor goes for a foul shot during overtime.

One method of capitalizing on the negatives from the crowd is to pre-pare yourself for it, well in advance and continuously throughout the season, by mental programming. Mentally program, through autosuggestion or self-hypnosis, that you have a mental converter system that automatically takes all negative crowd input and causes you to do better than ever. Think this idea through, then repeat it to yourself ten times each morning and again before retiring in the evening. Think of this procedure as reinforcing a self-administered posthypnotic suggestion. You will gain much benefit from it. Keep using this autosuggestion until the new reaction is automatic and feels permanent.

The suggestion is, "I have a converter system that takes all negative crowd input and causes me to perform better than ever."

Example 3

QUESTION: What causes slumps, and why are they so hard to break?

ANSWER: When you're hot, you're hot. When you're not, you're not! Thus it ever was. A hot streak seems to generate itself, and a slump does the same.

It doesn't matter what sport you are in, or whether it's individual or team competition.

In my opinion, most slumps are psychological. It is true that if training is broken, and rest and diet are interrupted, performance can be affected for the worse. But that kind of slump is usually correctible by getting back "with the program."

Generally, a mental slump is caused and continued because the player is trying too hard. He may be too critical or analytical about his technique and form. If, following an isolated "off" performance, you examine moves, position, and technique too closely, it can result in tension not normally present. This tension erodes the naturalness of performance that comes from weeks, months, and years of practice.

It is similar to what occurs when a pianist or typist begins thinking about what the fingers are doing. Instead of letting the fingers do their walking on their own, the fingers are walked—resulting in tightness, loss of spontaneity, naturalness, and accuracy. The same is true in athletics, whether it be golf, tennis, bowling, or whatever. When you pay too much attention to technique, it can be a self-perpetuating hindrance resulting in less effective performance.

This in turn can lead to more worry, such as, "What am I doing wrong? Why can't I do it right?" And, "Well, I hope I can do it this time." And finally, "I bet I mess it up again." If you don't expect to do well, you won't.

Concentration on what's wrong has a negative effect on an athlete, just as concentration on winning and success has a positive effect.

If a slump hits, learn to take a friendly attitude toward it. Treat it as a very brief visitor. Keep your thoughts centered on what's right about your play. Imagine the feelings that you enjoy when you're on a hot streak. Imagine those feelings so completely that you can feel them, and then proceed with a sense of *knowing* that you are on track again.

Example 4

QUESTION: How can I develop greater consistency? I know I can play well, but it's hard to be consistent at it. Have you some suggestions?

ANSWER: Being consistent in sports is possible through both physical and mental control. At the physical level, it requires that you maintain a consistent regimen of nutrition, rest, and training. Burning the midnight oil, deviating from your special diet, or slacking off in training before competition will have some bearing on reduced physical efficiency.

Those factors can also affect many athletes mentally by reducing mental efficiency, poise, and even self-confidence. A fatigued body and mind, for instance, result in increased tendency toward negative thought, attitudes, and feelings, which can make a significant difference in athletic performance.

Consistency can also be achieved by consciously selecting performance goals on a regular basis. Some athletes perform, then look to see how they've done. These tend to be less consistent. Others set regular goals, in effect deciding how they will do in advance, and then work toward achieving those performance goals. These athletes usually prove to be more consistent.

Consistency is also helped by daily mental conditioning. You can mentally program consistency through affirmation or autosuggestion. Say or think, "I am a superbly consistent athlete at all times." Repeat this ten or twenty times a day. Also use imagery; imagine yourself in a remarkable consistent manner. Imagine, in detail, looking over the various statistics of your performance three months from now. Envision a steady, consistent performance and growth.

Give considerable thought to defining exactly what you mean by being consistent. In your mind, apply your definition to all aspects of your sport. Be able to imagine and apply your meaning of being consistent to technique, timing, energy, attitude, confidence, etc.

If you are not clear, in depth, as to what you mean by being consistent, you will never achieve it. So be sure to devote some time to defining your meaning.

Example 5

QUESTION: I've been very fortunate to discover how much power our minds really have over our bodies in competitive performance. As a player, mental programming has worked wonders for me, especially in my golf game. But as a soccer coach, and using it "on" my players, the results have been only so-so. Any comments, please?

ANSWER: Yes, your description of your use of the principles of Mental Dynamics on yourself, and others, plus the difference in results, is very common. Furthermore, the answer to your problem is found in your statement about using it "on" your players.

The principles of Mental Dynamics *always* work better "on" people who are self-applying them. In fact, any obvious attempt at programming others may well be met with conscious or unconscious resistance. When mental programming of goals is done knowledgeably, and of free will, it inevitably will be more effective.

Here are two suggestions that will let Mental Dynamics work successfully with your players.

1. Let the use of Mental Dynamics principles and techniques be a joint, cooperative project between you and your players. Through individual "head" sessions, or in team meetings, work together with them to identify, select, and define goals. Once this is accomplished, explain to them that you will be helping them to achieve those goals by several mental programming systems, including affirming "at" them and putting signs around with goals on them to help keep them in mind.

2. A second preferred method is to teach them as much about the theory and techniques of Mental Dynamics as you can. Players who understand this mental power and how it works are usually excited about using it. And they will be grateful to you for explaining it, since they can use it to improve in other areas of their lives as well. Introduce them to this book or let them listen to the Mental Dynamics for Athletes Audio Cassette Tape Program.

As a coach, you are a teacher. Your players are there to learn. You give them the tools to help them to improve. This applies to the mind as well as to the body. The player who has the tools to work with will usually do a better job.

Example 6

Here's a question posed by a golfer preparing himself to go on the Pro Golf Tour.

QUESTION: I usually play a good consistent game and will shoot par for the first twelve to fifteen holes, then I putt one that just edges the lip of the hole and from there on my game goes downhill. One bogey after another. I check my stance, grip, swing, everything, but nothing works and before I know it, I start to steer the ball. Have you any suggestions?

ANSWER: Reading between the lines of your letter, I am inclined to think that you are letting one slight imperfection break your good concentration, causing you to go from automatic to manual control. To put it another way—from playing out of the subconscious to playing from the conscious mind. The difference is subtle, but significant.

Your statement that you shoot "a consistent game for the first twelve to fifteen holes" tells me that you are well trained and well practiced. As such you can "let yourself go" and play automatically—as in a trance—without thinking about all the details. Only the positive results you want. It's the same as a pianist or typist. When they are really humming, it is because they just let go and let the fingers do the walking.

When you make a slight error, though, you apparently shift gears into the conscious-thinking, analyzing conscious mind. You begin to analyze everything you do, and as a result you tense up and lose the flow, causing you to steer the ball. Just like the pianist or typist who tries to consciously direct each movement of each finger. You can well imagine the results of that.

Analyzing the problem may also result in visualizing what you don't want to happen and can cause you some minor negative programming, right there on the green.

Next time you play and an error occurs, try making a quick mental correction by simply seeing your next ball doing exactly what you want. Do not analyze or introspect—just see it do your bidding, in your mind. Assume the mental-emotional feelings you had during the earlier holes. Be kind to yourself and do not "get on" yourself for a slight error. Mentally picture a few birdies.

You might also mentally program the goal of playing consistently and maintaining perfect concentration throughout the entire match. Do this on a daily basis for a month.

15 Extra Innings

We all have dreams. But in order to make dreams into a reality, it takes an awful lot of determination, dedication, self-discipline, and effort. These things apply to everyday life. You learn not only the sport but things like respect of others, ethics in life, how you are going to live, how you treat your fellowman, how you live with your fellowman.

JESSE OWENS[1]

All events must eventually come to an end and our book is no exception. Yet, as in some sports, playing time can be extended through overtime or extra innings. Here we, too, would like to take advantage of that possibility and get in our overtime play.

USE YOUR MENTAL MAGIC

This book has been addressed to athletes, coaches, and other people in sports and recreation. It has presented many ideas, theories, philosophies, and how-to concepts that people can use to improve their sports performance. We like to think of it as mental magic, and we know that as you practice the methods taught, you will feel the same way.

But the most exciting thought to entertain is that since this mental magic will work in sports, then why not in all areas of life? After all, isn't sport just a microcosm of life itself? We think so. More than one philosopher has likened life to a great game.

The theory, philosophy, and techniques that you have learned in this book, though addressed to sports, are indeed applicable to all areas of your life. And we strongly suspect that as you learned these principles you already were mentally relating them to some nonsport part of your life. Our own experience has been that way. Many times, during the first hours of a full live Mental Dynamics for Athletes clinic, author Bennett will ask members of his group, "What benefits do you hope to gain for yourself as a result of this weekend session?" He would then write those suggestions on the blackboard,

146   [1] Frank Litsky, *Superstars* (Secaucus, N.J.: Derbibooks, Inc., 1975).

and more often than not, the number of nonsport benefits desired far out-numbered the sports-related benefits.

WHAT YOU THINK IS WHAT YOU FEEL

Do you remember what we said about the mental law of cause and effect? It is easy to see that this principle can be applied to every situation you encounter in the course of a day. *What you think is what you feel.* That is what the law of cause and effect means. What you think about yourself as a student, coach, business or professional person is going to strongly affect how you feel about yourself in those areas and also influence how effective you are in performing in those areas. The way you think about situations at home, in the family, and in the marriage are going to affect those relationships significantly.

How you think about yourself as a person or how you think about other people will always affect your life and your relationships in a major way. If you react with angry or resentful thoughts about your spouse's behavior, then that is how you will experience or realize your spouse. For when you think resentfully, the law of cause and effect will cause you to feel or experience resentment. Remember: *If you think caringly, you feel caringly.*

If your thoughts are depressing, then you feel depressed. Because of this law, it is impossible to think self-doubt and expect to feel self-confidence. It is impossible to think belittling thoughts about yourself or anyone else and not expect that you will also feel a loss of esteem, love, and respect.

When we decided to write this book, it was done with the idea of presenting a viable psychology for athletes, to help athletes. Yet in the back of our minds there was always the idea that when you learn these principles and apply them to sports first, you would then be able to transfer all of this to your whole life. Look further, then, at what we mean.

The principle of cause and effect is important not only to immediate situations but to your entire life as well. Ask yourself, "How do I want to experience my life as a whole? What kind of person do I want to evolve into? What kind of personality, career, family life do I want to experience over the *long haul?*" The Law of Cause and Effect says that *YOU, through your thoughts, are the creator of your own future, your own destiny.* Thought is the first cause and ultimately determines how you will experience your life in these and/or any other categories. *Therefore, in order to experience your life now and in the future as you would have it, train yourself always to keep your thoughts in harmony with that future.* This means not only thinking your goal but believing you can achieve it. Your thought, in the form of beliefs, attitudes, and self-images, must all be directed toward, and in harmony with, your goal.

This principle is well illustrated in the story told by Bob Richards, in his book *The Heart of a Champion*.[2] In it he relates how Olympic champion Charley Paddock would tell young people, in high school classes, "If you think you can, you can. If you believe a thing strongly enough, it can come to pass, in your life."

On one occasion, after saying this, he raised his hand and said, "Who knows but there is an Olympic champion here in this auditorium this afternoon."

Afterward, a skinny, spindle-legged youngster said to Mr. Paddock, "Gee, Mr. Paddock, I'd give anything if I could be an Olympic champion just like you." At that moment the boy's life changed. He had been inspired. He had a vision of his destiny. That skinny little boy went on to Berlin, Germany, in 1936, where he won four gold medals representing the United States in the Olympic Games.

This was Jesse Owens. When he returned home, he was paraded through the streets of Cleveland to the cheering of an adoring crowd. Occasionally his car stopped for him to sign autographs. With history repeating itself, another scrawny little kid pressed up to the car and yelled, "Gee, Mr. Owens, I'd give anything if I could be an Olympic champion just like you." Well, Mr. Owens reached over to this boy and said, "You know, young fellow, that was what I wanted to be when I was a little older than you are. If you'll work and train and believe, then you can become an Olympic champion."

Once again a young life was struck with inspiration and belief. Once again a young life changed. When that boy ran home, he immediately went to his grandmother and said, "Grandma, I'm going to be an Olympic champion!"

In 1948 this boy ran the 100-meter dash at the Olympic Games in London, England. Harrison ("Bones") Dillard not only won but tied Jesse Owens' Olympic record and later went on to break more world records.

These Olympic champions each had a goal, a vision. By keeping all their thoughts in harmony with that goal, they were able to achieve it and even go beyond.

Chapter 3, on "mind zapping," contains information that is just as important to your whole life as to your sport. Review those principles. When you understand hypnosis as being any situation that allows thought into the subconscious mind, reflect that you are *always in hypnosis* in one way or another.

Think of it. How many times a day or week do you describe yourself in a certain way to friends? "I am always forgetting names." "I just can't

[2] Bob Richard, *The Heart of a Champion* (Old Tappan, N.J.: Fleming H. Revell Co., 1960).

stay on my diet." "I just don't learn fast." "I must be destined to be poor." Through the important factor of repetition, these seemingly innocuous statements grow into unconscious belief systems which ultimately and subtly direct and control our lives.

Stop and think for a moment what seemingly innocent little phrases you think or speak from time to time. If your life hasn't progressed in certain areas as you feel you would like, perhaps you should monitor yourself for this kind of limiting self-hypnosis.

The repetition of a certain idea or thought frequently acts in the same way as an affirmation. Sooner or later we may all wind up affirming the very thing we don't want, and never realize that we are doing it.

As an example, author Bennett has been leading seminars for many years and prided himself on how well he helps his students achieve vivid, effective visualization. One evening, while returning home from work with a friend who had taken his course, the conversation came around to the subject of visualization. Bennett ruefully exclaimed, "I am envious of my students. I only wish I could visualize as well as they do. I never could visualize very well."

The teacher was put firmly in his place as his friend said, "Bennett, you are a fine one. I have heard you say that many times. Why are you affirming that you can't visualize?"

With that encounter, and tail between his legs, Bennett took the correction, established his new goal, and has been programming an incredible ability to visualize effectively any goal he wishes.

As you can see, it is easy to affirm the negative without realizing it. Some of it is habitual, and habits are things we often do unconsciously. Thus, it is all-important to become a good listener. Listen to yourself and make sure you are not hypnotizing (programming) yourself away from your desires.

In Chapter 3 we also mentioned the trance as an important condition of hypnosis—especially that kind of trance that we experience early in the morning and as we drift off to sleep at night.

We invite you to let these become special times in your life to be used for mentally programming not only athletic goals but goals of all kinds. What a wonderful time to program self-image and self-esteem goals. There is no more perfect time to set the "tone" or "spirit" for the day than first thing in the morning.

Awake in the morning and gently affirm to yourself, "It's great to be alive," or "Here I am world. Bring on your challenges." This can do more to set you on the right track than any other way we know. Remember, whether you affirm those words or others of your own choosing, at this time of morning they are going straight into the subconscious mind, and more often than not you will experience a very satisfying posthypnotic benefit throughout your day.

Fortunately, this is not an idea of ours that you need to believe in order to try. It's open for testing. Just try it and find out for yourself. Give it a fair trial, because if it really does work, you'll certainly want to know. Try it for one week. Each morning, upon arising, *repeat* some positive thought, idea, affirmation, or meditation. And then see if the general tone of your day or mood level isn't elevated.

MAN AS A GOAL-SETTING CREATURE

Of all living creatures, there is none that is better designed for creative or goal-striving activity than the human being. We humans have several things going for us that so far as we know, no other life form has. They are (1) imagination, (2) will, and (3) creative subconscious.

By using our imaginations we are able to conceive and define a goal. By employing our will we are able to pursue it. By engaging our creative subconscious we are enabled to achieve it. Goal setting and achieving in sports are exciting and worthwhile. Now apply the goal-setting principle to all of your life—you can imagine new goals in the area of personality, character, self-image, and self-esteem. You can conceive goals for yourself that relate to your lifetime career, family and marriage relationships, health and fitness, community and civic involvements. Your goals can be material, relating to home, car, or recreational equipment, or your goals may be entirely spiritual.

Whatever they are, you may apply the same principles and techniques that you learned for your sport goals. Exactly the same procedures are followed as outlined in Chapter 5. The mental programming is also the same, as in the affirmation and imagery. Not a thing is different, except the goals.

To stimulate your thinking about possible goals in nonsport areas of your life a suggested goals list can be found in the Appendix. An affirmation list that relates to this goals list and corresponds to it numerically can also be found in the Appendix.

And now as our overtime approaches an end, one final word regarding application of these principles to your life in general: *Study and restudy Chapter 7, "The Secret"*! This principle could be the most important one you ever learn.

How you regard yourself—how you value yourself—as a human being not only affects you in a major way with respect to your sport but is also a major influence on your success in family, love, studies, and career. It is a key factor in self-confidence. It is an essential ingredient for the enjoyment of life.

Use your self-esteem affirmation daily (see affirmation number one on the general affirmation list on page 162). In the same manner that you build physical strength, through regular exercise and conditioning, with a healthy well-conditioned self-esteem you can confidently meet and be victor over any competition, opponent, or antagonist in life generally.

The time clock is at an end now, and so we extend this last thought to you: As in sport—and all physical skills—practice of each technique and method brings forth excellence. You should practice each lesson in this book until you realize its value and achieve excellence in your own mental skills. Then keep on moving ahead. Take one step at a time—realize your sports goals and also your goals for life.

Be a winner in sports.
Be a winner in life!

Grieve not for me,
Who am about to start,
A new adventure.
Eager I stand,
And ready to depart,
Me and my reckless, pioneering heart!
Anon.

Appendix
Forms, Charts, and Lists

WORKSHEET

Dreams and Secret Wishes

SHORT TERM

Sports: _____

Career: _____

Family: _____

Other: _____

LONG TERM

Sports: _____

Career: _____

Family: _____

154   Other: _____

SUGGESTED GOALS LIST

Instructions: See Chapter 5 for use of this list. When self-survey is complete, choose goals based on ratings of 1 to 5 first. Then choose goals based on ratings of 6+.

Mental

1. To have superb self-confidence.
2. To have powerful concentration.
3. To be able to relax (loosen up) at will.
4. To be self-motivating.
5. To accept coaching and teaching from coaches.
6. To welcome constructive criticism.
7. To handle unfair criticism easily.
8. To not be intimidated by other players (opponents).
9. To have rapport with my audiences.
10. To be relaxed with "away" fans.
11. To be relaxed with the press.
12. To handle negative press.
13. To be extremely adaptable.
14. To be in emotional control at all times.
15. To handle what seems to be inept or incorrect officiating.
16. To have a superb memory.
17. To always maintain great determination.
18. To accept responsibility for my shortcomings and my successes.
19. To never be negatively affected by bad breaks, bad calls, or mistakes.
20. To play better because of bad breaks, bad calls, or mistakes.
21. To be mentally tough (see goal 20).
22. To develop exceptional decision-making ability.
23. To have immunity to being "psyched out."

General

24. To maintain a superb self-image as an athlete.
25. To maintain a superb self-image as a person.
26. To master all official rules.
27. To master game strategy.
28. To be creative and resourceful.
29. To learn rapidly and comprehensively.
30. To enjoy the role of leadership.
31. To be free to speak up for my beliefs.
32. To physically adjust positively to situations, e.g., climate, altitude, jet lag, "away" areas, sudden switches in plans, locations, dates, etc.
33. To enjoy all aspects of my sport.
34. To be able to read the opposition.
35. To practice good sportsmanship.
36. To have an effective monitor and converter system.
37. To know and understand my sports equipment completely.

Team

38. To have excellent rapport with my teammates.
39. To share a superb team self-image.
40. To always praise and encourage teammates.
41. To accept the authority of coaches, captains, rules, etc.
42. To place the good of the team above personal ambition.
43. To trust coaches and teammates.
44. To have pride in my team.
45. To have and inspire team loyalty and unity.

Ability

46. To master techniques of my sport, e.g., shooting, batting, fielding, throwing, serving, etc.
47. To raise my shooting, batting, fielding, etc. average this year by ____%.
48. To be a superb defensive player (strategist).
49. To be a superb offensive player (strategist).
50. To set and achieve and maintain high athletic goals.
51. To be more aggressive in play.
52. To be quick and alert in all actions and reactions.
53. To be steady and sure in all actions and reactions.

Conditioning

54. To enjoy practice, conditioning, and drill work.
55. To practice "mentals" regularly.
56. To give maximum effort at all times.
57. To have fantastic physical endurance.
58. To have superb recovery and ability to reenergize myself physically and mentally.
59. To have control over pain.
60. To be able to speed up healing.
61. To practice each new drill or exercise until perfected.

Personal

62. To always conduct myself at the highest moral and ethical levels.
63. To have good relationships with all my family members.
64. To have an ever-growing healthy self-esteem.

Goals Suggested by Coaches

65.
66.
67.

Other

AFFIRMATIONS

Mental

1. I always enjoy complete and total self-confidence.
2. I am always able to apply powerful concentration as conditions require.
3. I am able to relax at any chosen level anytime.
4. I especially enjoy being self-directed and self-motivated at all times.
5. I always welcome guidance and instruction from my coaches.
6. I am always open and responsive to constructive criticism or advice.
7. I am completely oblivious and unaffected by unfair criticisms or put-downs.
8. I am never intimidated by the thoughts or opinions of other people. (*Alternates:* I am totally immune to "psyching-out" efforts of my opponents. I always feel confident and self-assured when in the presence of my opponents.)
9. I always enjoy good rapport with my audiences.
10. I am always relaxed and at ease with the "away" fans.
11. I am always relaxed and at ease with members of the press.
12. I have complete mental immunity to negative press (see affirmation 36 regarding converter).
13. I am always extremely flexible and adjustable.
14. I always enjoy maintaining emotional control.
15. I always adjust speedily to what seems to be inept or inaccurate officiating.
16. I have a superb memory and an uncanny ability to recall data as needed.
17. I always enjoy being a superbly determined person.
18. I always accept responsibility for my shortcomings and my successes.
19. I always maintain a positive attitude even after bad breaks, bad calls, or mistakes.
20. I am so constituted that I always play even better after bad breaks, bad calls, or mistakes.
21. I enjoy being a person of exceptional mental toughness.
22. I always make the right decision at the right time.
23. I am totally immune to being "psyched out" by players or situations.

General

24. I always enjoy a superbly positive view of myself as an athlete.
25. I always maintain a superb view of myself as a person.
26. I have mastered all of the rules of my sport.
27. I have completely mastered all of the game strategy of my sport.
28. I enjoy being a superbly creative and resourceful person.
29. I enjoy learning rapidly and comprehensively.
30. I especially enjoy being a leader among my peers.
31. I am always free to respectfully speak up for my beliefs.
32. I have a fantastic ability to physically adjust positively to all situations, for instance, altitude, climate, jet lag, sudden switches in plans, locations, dates, etc.

33. I thoroughly enjoy all aspects of my sport.
34. I especially enjoy being good at reading the opposition.
35. I take pride in practicing good sportsmanship.
36. I have a completely effective monitor and converter system.
37. I thoroughly know and understand all of my sports equipment.

Team

38. I thoroughly enjoy good "vibes" with all of my teammates.
39. I especially enjoy sharing a superb team self-image with all my teammates.
40. I always praise and encourage each one of my teammates.
41. In thought, action, and speech I always accept the authority of my coaches, captains, and rules.
42. I always place the welfare and the good of my team above personal ambition.
43. I have complete confidence and trust in all my coaches and teammates.
44. I enjoy, with pride, being a member of my team.
45. I have strong feelings of team loyalty and unity and because of this I inspire the same in other team members.

Ability

46. I am mastering the unique techniques of my sport, e.g., shooting, batting, fielding, throwing, serving, etc.
47. This year I am raising my shooting, batting, fielding, etc., average by ___%.
48. I especially enjoy being a superb defensive player, and have mastered defensive strategies.
49. I especially enjoy being a superb offensive player, and have mastered offensive strategies.
50. I always enjoy setting, achieving, and maintaining high athletic goals.
51. I always enjoy playing aggressively and with enthusiasm.
52. I enjoy being quick and alert in all my actions and reactions.
53. I especially enjoy being sure in all my actions and reactions.

Conditioning

54. I always enjoy practicing, conditioning, and drilling with maximum effectiveness.
55. I especially enjoy practicing my "mentals" regularly.
56. I always enjoy giving maximum effort at all times.
57. I always enjoy fantastic physical endurance.
58. I always have superb recovery and the ability to reenergize myself physically, at will.
59. I am growing in my ability to control pain.
60. I enjoy being able to accelerate the healing processes in the body. (*Alternate:* Health and healing flow to me and through me at all times.)
61. I always practice each new technique, drill, exercise, or strategy until perfected.

Personal

62. I always conduct myself at the highest moral and ethical levels.
63. I have superb relationships with all my family members.
64. I have an ever-growing healthy self-esteem and I like myself unconditionally.

Goals Suggested by Coaches

65.
66.
67.

Other

STARTER SHEET FOR DEFINING GOALS

GOAL _____

With this goal achieved I will feel _____

With this goal achieved I will act _____

With this goal achieved I will look _____

With this goal achieved I will think _____

With this goal achieved I will be _____

With this goal achieved I will perform _____

Other items of importance to understanding fully what I wish to achieve with this goal _____

_____

_____

_____

Summary of definition of goal (write out exactly what you have in mind and hope to see happen when this goal is realized).

ADDITIONAL GOALS FOR LIFE ENRICHMENT

Direction setting is the next natural step upon identifying unwanted factors in one's life or upon noting factors desired but absent from one's life. Here are some commonly used objectives.

Prerequisites to Good Living and Adjustment

1. To know my value as a person.
2. To maintain a positive self-image at all times.
3. To be at peace with my fellowman.
4. To feel truly alive.
5. To be a self-directed, self-governed person and to respect the right of others to be the same.

Marriage and Family Goals—Personal Growth

6. To have a good relationship with all my family members.
7. To be a more loving person.
8. To be free to express my love.
9. To think and act for myself without fear or anxiety.
10. To free myself from depression or black moods.
11. To free myself from anxiety.
12. To enjoy parenthood.
13. To be an effective parent.
14. To be relaxed with people.
15. To shake free from ghosts from the past.

Habits

16. To stop smoking.
17. To control weight.
18. To control eating habits.
19. To eliminate procrastination.
20. To stop swearing.

Career Goals

21. To enjoy my occupation.
22. To improve relationships with persons at work.
23. To be good at my job.
24. To have a larger income.
25. To acquire certain items: home, boat, etc.
26. To recognize my limitless possibilities.
27. To be relaxed about money and material possessions.
28. To work with less pressure.

Personal Achievement Goals

29. To be organized.
30. To be neat.
31. To be poised.
32. To improve memory.
33. To improve reading skills.
34. To finish tasks efficiently and promptly.
35. To develop good thought habits and self-mastery.
36. To be adept at solving problems and creative thinking.
37. To be a good speaker.
38. To make decisions easily.

Health Goals

39. For quick recuperation.
40. For relief of pain or discomfort.
41. For better sleep habits.
42. For ability to draw on vital reserves ("second wind").
43. For good sense of well-being.
44. For elimination of tension headaches.

Leisure Time Goals

45. To make the most of free time.
46. To improve in sports.
47. To improve in the arts.
48. To enjoy leisure without guilt.

Spiritual Goals

49. To know God.
50. To understand my beliefs.
51. To acquire deeper spiritual experience and insight.
52. To involve myself in service to others.

(Other goals are based on individual need and desire.)

Special Goals

53. To maintain habit of mental programming.
54. To establish and maintain friendships.
55. To be at ease with my friends.
56. To establish a monitor system.

LIFE ENRICHMENT AFFIRMATIONS

"When you have envisioned a goal and created its attainment on the plane of the mind, nothing can stop you from realizing that goal but the creation of your failure on the plane of your mind."[1]

Basic Affirmations:
Prerequisites to
Good Living and Adjustment

1. I am especially happy to be _____ and I like myself without condition.
2. I enjoy a positive self-image at all times and in all situations.
3. I always give unconditional value to everyone I meet.
4. Every day, in every respect, I feel great physically, emotionally, mentally, and spiritually.
5. I enjoy being a self-directed person and I respect the right of others to be self-directed.

Affirmations Highly Beneficial
to Family and Marriage Relations
and Personal Growth

6. I especially love and enjoy _____ and I never devalue

   _____ by destructive criticism or labels.
7. I always show appreciation and gratitude as a first step in becoming a truly loving person.

8. I am completely free to express my love to _____ in every way (helpfulness, verbally, physically, etc.).
9. I am never intimidated by the thoughts or opinions of any other person.
10. I never withdraw or brood when things don't go to my liking.
11. I reject all thought that results in fear. I reject fear.

[1]U.S. Anderson, *Three Magic Words* (New York: Elsevier-Dutton Publishing Co., Inc., 1954).

162

12. I especially enjoy being a superb parent.
13. I take pride in being an effective parent.
14. I am relaxed and at ease at all times with all people.
15. The ghosts of the past are rendered harmless now.

Affirmations for Eliminating Unwanted Habits

16. I enjoy being a nonsmoker. I never smoke and I have no desire to smoke.

17. I weigh _____ pounds and enjoy excellent health. I feel fit all the time.
18. I have a (lively/moderate) appetite and can easily control the amount of food I consume. (*Alternate:* I enjoy eating the food I need, no more,

    no less, to weigh _____ pounds.)
19. I take pride in getting things done right away, and enjoy the extra free time I have because of it.
20. My language is always pleasant, appealing, and presentable to all people.

Affirmations Helpful to Career Goals

21. I especially enjoy all facets of my occupation as _____.
22. I am unusually tactful and able in my dealings with all my customers, clients, superiors, subservients, co-workers, etc.
23. I truly delight in keeping myself superbly knowledgeable and skillful in all areas of my occupation.

24. My yearly income is _____.
25. I have a home, boat, car, camper, etc.
26. I am always grateful for the great abundance that exists in the world.
27. I am relaxed and at peace with respect to money needs and material possessions.
28. I especially enjoy working in such a manner that pressure and tension are things of the past. (*Alternate*: I take delight in overcoming obstacles in the path of my goals.)

Affirmations Helpful in Personal Achievement

29. I am most efficient and effective in all my daily activities because of my superb ability to organize all that I do.
30. I am neat and orderly in my thinking and in all of my habits.
31. I present myself at all times as calm, deliberate, and with authority.
32. I have an excellent memory and an uncanny ability to recall data as needed.

33. My reading speed is _____ w.p.m. and I have exceptional comprehension and retention.

34. I delight in completing every task I begin.
35. I use my affirmations and imagery every day and delight in finding them becoming increasingly effective.
36. I make daily use of the creative and problem solving power of my subconscious.
37. I am an effective speaker, knowledgeable, convincing, and relaxed.
38. I always make decisions quickly and easily.

Affirmations Beneficial to Health

39. Every day in every respect my _____ is getting better.
40. Every day in every respect the pain is going.
41. I am able to go to sleep easily and waken alert and refreshed.
42. I possess great reserves of strength and energy and can summon them on command.
43. I feel physically fit at all times.
44. I am especially able to make tension headaches cease.

Affirmations for Activities

45. I always enjoy my leisure time to the utmost.
46. I am a superb tennis player, bowler, golfer, swimmer, skier, climber, etc.
47. I am a superb artist, writer, musician, decorator, singer, etc.
48. I especially enjoy and deserve my leisure time without any sense of guilt.

Affirmations for Spiritual Growth

49. I grow closer to God every day.
50. I especially enjoy reading and studying in my faith.
51. I am always open to the love and wisdom of my creator.
52. I enjoy giving of my time and energy to others in need.
    (Other affirmations may be written to meet a specific need.)

Affirmations for Special Occasions

53. I especially enjoy affirming and using imagery each and every day.
54. I enjoy establishing and maintaining lasting and meaningful friendships.
55. I have great freedom to truly express my thoughts and feelings among my friends.
56. I have a monitor system that alerts me when I use negative thinking, or when my thoughts run counter to my goals.

SAMPLE TIME SCHEDULE FOR MENTAL PROGRAMMING SESSIONS

		SUN.	MON.	TUES.	WED.	THUR.	FRI.	SAT.
A.M. SESSION	START TIME							
	END TIME							
	ELAPSED TIME							
P.M. SESSION	START TIME							
	END TIME							
	ELAPSED TIME							
TOTAL ELAPSED TIME								

NOTE: See Chapter 12 for details on the use of this schedule.

165

THE MIRACLE OF SPORTS PSYCHOLOGY was based on the audio cassette, mental conditioning program, entitled Mental Dynamics for Athletes. The audio training program, written and produced by James Bennett, includes all the relaxation and mental programming exercises provided in this book. Readers who would like further information or may wish to acquire the Mental Dynamics for Athletes audio cassette program may write to:

Mental Dynamics for Athletes
P. O. Box 10185
Bainbridge Island, WA 98110

Index